scenes from

postmodern life

Cultural Studies of the Americas

Edited by George Yúdice, Jean Franco, and Juan Flores

scenes from
postmodern life

Beatriz Sarlo

Translated by
Jon Beasley-Murray

Cultural Studies of the Americas — Volume 7

University of Minnesota Press

Minneapolis — London

Originally published as *Escenas de la vida posmoderna,* copyright
1994 Compañía Editora Espasa Calpe Argentina S.A.

Published by the University of Minnesota Press
111 Third Avenue South, Suite 290
Minneapolis, MN 55401-2520
http://www.upress.umn.edu

Library of Congress Cataloging-in-Publication Data

Sarlo, Beatriz.
    [Escenas de la vida posmoderna. English]
    Scenes from postmodern life / Beatriz Sarlo ; translated by
Jon Beasley-Murray.
        p.   cm. (Cultural studies of the Americas ; v. 7)
    Includes bibliographical references.
    ISBN 0-8166-3008-9 (HC : alk. paper) — ISBN 0-8166-3009-7
(PB : alk. paper)
    1. Argentina—Civilization—1955–   2. Arts—Argentina.
3. Television broadcasting—Social aspects—Argentina.
4. Intellectuals—Argentina.   I. Title.   II. Series.
    F2849.2 .S22813 2001
    982.03'5—dc21
                                                    2001004001

Printed in the United States of America on acid-free paper

The University of Minnesota is an equal-opportunity educator and
employer.

11 10 09 08 07 06 05 04 03 02 01   10 9 8 7 6 5 4 3 2 1

Contents

Translator's Introduction
In Argentina

Beatriz Sarlo is without doubt one of the most significant intellectuals working in Latin America today. She is professor of Argentine literature at the University of Buenos Aires, director of the journal *Punto de Vista,* and author of numerous books and articles on topics that range from nineteenth-century literature to contemporary avant-garde film. With her work on *Punto de Vista,* and with collaborators such as the critic Carlos Altamirano and the novelist Ricardo Piglia, she tested the limits of what could be said during Argentina's military dictatorship, and has since helped set the terms for intellectual debate during the democratic transition and neoliberal revolution that have followed. With her articles and books that have been published and distributed throughout the region and elsewhere, she has contributed to defining and consolidating the increasingly important field of Latin American cultural studies.

Sarlo is at ease as much in the United States or the United Kingdom as in her native Buenos Aires, in English as much as in Spanish, and with Anglophone and continental European traditions as much as with Argentine literary and cultural history. She has been a visiting professor or researcher at, among other universities, Columbia, Berkeley, and Cambridge; she has been influenced by authors such as Theodor Adorno, Raymond Williams, and Pierre Bourdieu, and has also intervened in the debates that have arisen from these authors' works, debates about cultural studies, postmodernity, and the role of the intellectual. Throughout, however, she has always been concerned with what it means to be an Argentine intellectual, not only rereading the canon of Argentine texts and authors and analyzing Argentine cultural history, but also often taking a very prominent stand in the public and political life of her country. Sarlo's significance, in other words, is in part due to her ability to translate ideas and arguments (in both directions) between a specific national context and a transnational intellectual community. As such, it is only surprising that more of her books have not been translated into English before now.

Yet Sarlo is well aware of the conflicts and complexities that haunt cultural translation. Elsewhere, in a book devoted to an analysis of what she terms the machinery of culture, Sarlo examines the pitfalls as well as the possibilities inherent in the translations effected by another prestigious Argentine journal, *Sur,* and its director, Victoria Ocampo. Financed largely by Ocampo's own money, and impelled by her energy for bringing people together, from the 1930s to the 1960s *Sur* introduced to Latin America the writings of figures such as André Malraux, Albert Camus, and Jean-Paul Sartre, while also providing a showcase for Argentine writers, above all Jorge Luis Borges. Yet Sarlo argues that Ocampo, who herself always wrote in French, which she then translated into Spanish, fell into the trap of imagining all culture to be commensurable, and that all differences could be annulled through translation. When, inevitably, misunderstanding and conflict arose in her dealings with European intellectuals, Ocampo was not equipped to deal with the humiliation and disappointment that ensued.

If Ocampo was archetypically modern in her faith in the power of a universalist, cosmopolitan discourse to make cultural difference ultimately irrelevant, Sarlo here shows her postmodern inflection at the outset by stressing the specificity of the place from which she speaks. Her first sentence declares, "Here we are . . . in Argentina." The book as a whole then investigates the implications of writing from a *particular* per-

spective about *general* concerns. Sarlo analyzes the ways in
which the sense of a common discourse that would bridge differences such as those between the national and the international, high culture and mass culture, or public and private
has tended to disappear in the transition from modernity to
postmodernity, only to reappear in new guise. Sarlo is as skeptical of the claim that in postmodernity the mass media and
globalization offer a new "common culture" as she is of the
notion that modernity's sense of commonality could ever be
taken for granted. Yet she insists that there is no use giving up
and abandoning this question: The negotiation between commonality and difference should still be high on our political
agenda.

What does it mean to be "in Argentina"? Argentina's founding political myth is that of the urgent choice between "civilization or barbarism," between European refinement or what
Borges called the "South American destiny" of atavism, desire, and violence. Underlying and structuring this myth is an
anxiety that Argentina is in fact neither civilized nor (suitably,
exotically) barbaric—in other words, that, whatever choices
Argentina may make, civilization and barbarism, sameness
and difference will always cohabit somewhat uneasily. Faced
with the violence and the civilized, modern barbarism of the
military regime that governed the country in the period from
1976 to 1983, Sarlo and her collaborators on *Punto de Vista*
returned to the founding texts of Argentine literature and politics to rethink these myths and anxieties and so also, indirectly, to construct resources for thinking about the contemporary
situation. One result of this detour through the nineteenth
century forced on Sarlo by the exigencies of censorship and
clandestinity was the reconceptualization of this anxiety as an
advantage. If Argentine culture was both international, cosmopolitan ("civilized") and local, provincial ("barbaric"), this
cut both ways. As Sarlo would later say of Borges, a writer
who during the 1960s and 1970s had been despised by the
third-worldist and nationalist Argentine Left not only for his

political views but also for his valorization of European high culture: His cosmopolitanism enables him to reinvent Argentine literature, while "by reinventing a national tradition, [he] also offers Argentine national culture an oblique reading of Western literatures." It is this oblique relation to the West that means "there is no writer in Argentine literature more Argentine than Borges." Sarlo takes this same oblique stance toward postmodernity.

"In Argentina," the "social landscape . . . is recognizably part of the Western world," while at the same time it exhibits certain illuminating differences or deviations from the model to which those of us in the "first world" are accustomed. These differences may be subtle: They may be a matter of contrast—above all, in that "here the contrasts are extreme." The Argentine mall culture that Sarlo describes, for instance, is part of a phenomenon prevalent throughout the world, and part of a process of "Los Angelization" whereby often international architectural firms replicate models first tested in the United States or Europe, which are then filled with globally identifiable chains and brands: "There is a way in which all shopping centers are the same." Yet, as Sarlo points out, the mall depends not simply on pointing up its participation in global consumer culture, but also on turning its back on the city in which it is situated; in Argentina, that divide between the mall and what surrounds it is all the more extreme. Though the mall tries to relocate its customers in an elsewhere in which geography and history would be erased, in Argentina that relocation is all the more clearly a dislocation, constituting a process of exclusion and symbolic violence.

Sarlo is here tracing the contours of what could be called a "peripheral postmodernity," just as earlier she had examined Buenos Aires's "peripheral modernity" of the 1920s and 1930s. To read the transition from modernity to postmodernity at the periphery reveals that postmodernity has no special prerogative over globalization. The shape of Argentina's modernity was heavily determined by the massive immigration from southern and eastern Europe that immediately preceded the period Sarlo studies. These immigrants brought with them their experiences, memories, and cultural practices and also impelled an extremely rapid urbanization and expansion of the cultural market for the newspapers, magazines, and serial novels that Sarlo analyzes. This immigration and cultural and social renovation led to Argentine culture being above all a *"culture of mixture . . .* in which cultural traits typical of the traditional elite persist at the same time as there is a huge process of importation of commodities, discourses, and symbolic practices."* When it comes to *Scenes from Postmodern Life,* then, Sarlo notes how peripheral modernity in some ways prefigures postmodernity, but she is equally concerned that those who make comparisons between (for example) postmodernity's soap operas and modernity's serial novels should know as much about serial novels (to which she has dedicated another book-length study) as they know about soap operas.

No doubt, whether in modernity or in postmodernity, many of the cultural similarities between the periphery and the global center (whether Europe or the United States) are a function of the postcolonial desire to imitate or reproduce trends that originate first in Paris, London, or New York. Often such imitation is seen as a double degradation: It contaminates third world culture while producing only a pale shadow of the culture that is imitated. In either case, authenticity is said to be compromised. At the periphery, nationalist critics of globalization lament the ways in which local traditions are changed or erased. At the center, the common (Eurocentric) assumption is that nothing of interest can come from the South. Sarlo, however, turns her position at the periphery of a globalizing world system to advantage by pointing out the ways in which, in Argentina, certain tendencies become evident that would elsewhere be missed; these tendencies have as much to do with our postmodernity as they do with hers.

For even mimicry, as some postcolonial critics have also argued (and as Borges allegorizes in his "Pierre Menard"), holds the power to surprise; even the most slavish repetition of the same will also introduce what may turn out to be a rather unnerving difference. Argentina (and perhaps especially Buenos Aires) provides a particularly good refutation of the argument, shared by cultural nationalism and Eurocentrism alike, that imitation entails degradation. Other Latin Americans are often quick to point out that Argentines have always been unusually attentive to fashions and trends originating elsewhere. Many jokes play on the apparent loss of national identity that may seem to ensue, such as the one that states that the only difference between an Uruguayan and an Argentinian is that an Argentinian is an Uruguayan who has been to Paris. But, in the first place, this same attentiveness ironically (as the joke itself indirectly suggests) helps to mark Argentine national identity, a point also made by Sarlo elsewhere in a discussion of the influential early-nineteenth-century poet-intellectual Esteban Echeverría and his journey to Paris and back. In the second place, the eagerness with which European and U.S. trends are reproduced in Argentina often means that they are found there in an accentuated and exaggerated form. Such has been the enthusiasm for the theories of the seemingly quintessentially French psychoanalyst Jacques Lacan, for instance, that there are now more Lacanian analysts in Buenos Aires than there are in the whole of France. Similarly, today plastic surgery is more prevalent in the Argentine capital than it is in Los Angeles or New York (or in any other country in the world). Sarlo here embarks on a series of reflections that derives from this uncanny amplification (rather than degradation or diminution) that imitation entails. Thanks to hyperreal or hyperfaithful mimicry, in Argentina the consequences of what is initiated elsewhere can be more clearly and starkly visible.

Cultural mimicry at the periphery, allied with the failure or absence of programs of economic redistribution, entails then especially an accentuation of the differences that also pervade the metropolitan center. The third world (and perhaps especially Latin America) is often either celebrated or condemned as a "land of contrasts." It is condemned for its contrasts of rich and poor, for the fact that destitution and crumbling public services exist side by side with immense wealth and a booming private sector. Sarlo echoes this condemnation insofar as she refuses the neoliberal mantra that claims that profits from stock-market booms or the revenue circulating as a result of the consumerism of the few will somehow trickle down to the millions who are struggling to survive in the countryside or in the urban informal economy. At the same time, however, rather than simplistic denunciation that lays the entire blame for such inequality at the door of (for instance) corruption on the part of the local elite, she prefers a systematic analysis of the way in which the global economy and transnational cultural and social trends combine to construct an international system of hierarchies and contrasts.

On the other hand, Latin America is celebrated (and sold) as a series of "lands of contrasts" by a strange alliance of the travel industry and culturalist romantics who point to geographical extremes (from glaciers to beaches, rain forests to pampas) and a cultural patchwork (traces of traditional and indigenous culture coexisting with post-Fordist industry or high-tech consumption) to produce the image of an exotic smorgasbord to delight the traveler, whether that be the long-haul tourist or the cultured reader of "magical realist" literature. This celebration of contrast is a fetishism of difference (and, indeed, in the case of commentary on magical realism, also a projection of that fetishism into Latin American culture; so Laura Esquivel, for instance, is read as providing a legitimation for a more general sentimental attachment to the exotic, dressed up as cultural refinement). It also involves a suspension of critique. Sarlo refuses such celebration; her point throughout is that Argentina is "like almost everywhere else in the West," albeit sometimes more so, and sometimes less so. If, in Argentina, difference is marked by intensity, and by the extravagance of certain contrasts, this intensity is no exotic "Latin spirit." Difference, for Sarlo, is the occasion for critique even when it is not the object of critique.

Sarlo offers an alternative to the celebrations and lamentations of postmodernity found elsewhere. She can do this because, in Argentina, she takes an oblique approach to the political issues at stake, an approach filtered through Argentina's political history and also through her own history of cultural and political engagement.

Twentieth-century Argentine political history is dominated by Peronism and by the reactions that Peronism elicited. (And as Sarlo indicates in her discussion of Evita as Argentina's first television icon, Peronism also dominates twentieth-century Argentina's cultural history.) Juan Perón governed for ten years from 1945, with Evita an icon by his side until her early death in 1952, and with the support of the overwhelming majority of Argentina's working class, before being overthrown by a military coup. Over the next twenty-five years, and although Peronism was proscribed and Perón was in exile in Spain, the political sphere was haunted by the legacy of his rule and by whispers of his possible return. If populism's claim is to be all things to all people, from Madrid and exercising influence without responsibility Perón could encourage a variety of groups with very divergent aims to think that he could be their salvation, too. In particular, many on the increasingly radicalized Left and many young people inspired by the Cuban revolution and third-worldist ideologies united under the banner of Peronism, and some, such as the *montoneros,* formed guerrilla groups that would fight under that banner. Others on the Left, some of whom also took up arms, were violently opposed to Perón, albeit equally opposed to the military regime of the time. The situation became still more complicated when Perón finally did return in 1973, repudiated the Peronist Youth, died after only a few months in the presidency, and left power in the hands of his second wife, Isabel, who was surrounded by the most unsavory of Peronist right-wing elements. Peronism and the Left were both split along a variety of lines, and the result was increasing violence as well as economic collapse. In 1976, another coup brought a military junta to power whose aim was to eradicate subversion and presumed subversion by any means possible, and who initiated the so-called dirty war in which thirty thousand people were killed or disappeared. This regime renounced power only in 1983, in the wake of Argentina's humiliating defeat in the war with Britain over the Falkland/Malvinas islands.

By the early 1970s, Sarlo was heavily involved with the non-Peronist radical Left and, along with a group (including Altamirano and Piglia) associated with the Revolutionary Communist Party and the Communist Vanguard party, edited the cultural journal *Los Libros* ("books"), whose theoretical agenda was influenced by Lacan and Althusser. However, as the Revolutionary Communists grew closer to Isabel Perón's government, this group distanced themselves from the journal, before it was closed by the military in 1976. Sarlo now writes about this period as something of a political and theoretical dead end, particularly insofar as aesthetics (and questions of cultural form) came to be subordinated absolutely to politics (and the question of reproducing the correct ideological line).

The most bloody years of the dictatorship were 1976–78, a period during which any cultural or political activity, such as a reading or discussion group, had to take place in conditions of utmost clandestinity. Sarlo recounts that by 1978 and after the soccer World Cup hosted by Argentina, there appeared to be some slight opening, and, with the help of Communist Vanguard, Sarlo and her group founded *Punto de Vista* ("point of view," on the basis that all had a right to their point of view). Under the conditions of dictatorship, Sarlo and others contributed articles under pseudonyms, and the journal had to subordinate politics to aesthetics, or rather to approach politics obliquely, through a rereading of the Argentine literary canon and cultural history. As such, the journal's editorial team became increasingly interested in critics such as Raymond Williams, Richard Hoggart, and Pierre Bourdieu, who seemed to offer the resources for this historical analysis and also indirectly to suggest ways of thinking about the conditions of possibility for the construction of public space and public debate.

In the early 1980s, as it became easier to believe that the dictatorship's days really were numbered (and as *Punto de*

Vista finally felt able to publish an editorial and its contributors able to write under their own names), the journal had to rethink its future within the context of a transition to democracy. It became clear that for most of those connected to the journal there would be no return to the revolutionary Marxist positions taken in the 1960s and 1970s, and Sarlo was one of those who moved most obviously to a position closer to social democracy, though she, along with a group of returning exiles, helped found the *Club de Cultura Socialista* ("club for socialist culture"). Around the time of the election of the neo-Peronist Carlos Menem in 1989, whose economic policies were neoliberal but whose rhetoric traded on the legacy of Peronism, and as can be seen in *Scenes from Postmodern Life,* Sarlo had identified the major objects of her critique to be neopopulism and neoliberalism, rather than capitalism tout court. By the 1990s, she was a political advisor to Frepaso (a new center-left political alliance formed in the wake of Menem's victory), particularly to Frepaso's senator and candidate for governor of Buenos Aires province, Graciela Fernández Meijide, a former human rights leader.

Thus in the background of Sarlo's critique of neopopulism, which elsewhere she associates with cultural studies and implicitly also with the U.S. academy, is an entire history of Argentine populism. Twentieth-century Argentina has lived through or in the shadow of the most thorough-going and successful experiments in political populism—although a corollary of Peronism's success was that it was also the most unsuccessful of populisms, and that it led to the great national disaster of the 1976 military coup and the dirty war. This instability, indeed, is a key characteristic of populism: At its most successful, it is also only ever a short step away from calamity; in populism, success and failure almost coincide. The aim or endpoint of populism is to produce the country as an absolutely homogenous unit, a cross-class alliance that admits no contradictions, presided over by a transcendent State personified by the populist leader. While temporary or limited

alliances are always possible, the closer that a populist movement comes to achieving its absolutist goal, the more it touches
upon a breaking point, a point at which the repressed differences reassert themselves. This return of the repressed was exactly what happened in Argentina in the early 1970s, when the
tensions between the left-wing Peronist Youth and the institutional defenders of the Peronist State exploded into violence
and created a vacuum into which the military intervened.
Populism promises and claims to create a common space and a
common culture, but its only answer to social contradictions
and tensions is to gloss over them with the sleight of hand that
points to a phantasmatic enemy elsewhere (the oligarchy,
international capital, or, in fascist variants, a stigmatized racial group such as the Jews).

For Sarlo, neopopulism is equally an empty gesture that
promises an empty community; simply, where classical populism stressed the State and the caudillo (or the caudillo's wife)
and his love for the people as the site of this imaginary reconciliation, neopopulism asks us to put our faith in the market
and its invisible hand. In either case, populism old or new demands that its subjects surrender their critical faculty for a de-
pendence on an affective investment, whether that affect be
cathected to the State and its public spectacle or to the com-
modity and the private spectacle of a televisual fantasy.

Sarlo's critique of neoliberalism is similarly uncompromising. She argues that neoliberalism is the mirror image of neopopulism in that it aims to exclude affect entirely from its discourse of technical planning. Neoliberal expertise produces a
"desensitized environment" in which questions of value are
redundant and intellectuals become simply technocrats. Her
attitude to traditional liberalism is more ambivalent. Indeed,
here lies what is perhaps the crux of this book. While Sarlo's
argument often flirts with a nostalgia for the heyday of the liberal intelligentsia, when intellectuals were both respected and
critical public figures, she is equally aware of the impossibility
of such a return. On the other hand, while Sarlo is acute in her
critiques of postmodern phenomena such as zapping and video

games, it is also clear that she is drawn to the intensity of feeling and participation that such phenomena offer, as a refuge from what is otherwise the sterility of neoliberal society. Her prose style reflects this enthusiasm, and the occasional conflicts between style and content that result manifest the extent to which her argument remains finely balanced between an optimistic belief in the possibility of transcending particularity and a half-feared, half-enthralled desire to explore the possibilities of more deterritorialized flows.

It is no coincidence that the one concept that resists translation in *Scenes from Postmodern Life* should be the most crucial concept. The Spanish word *público* is used to mean both public (as in "public sphere") and audience (as in a television program's audience). I have generally translated it as "viewing public." Sarlo's wager is that the expansion and proliferation of audiences within postmodernism may also provide the occasion for the reconstruction of a public sphere in which politics could be the subject of informed and critical debate. Her fear, however, is that the fragmentation of the public represented by the proliferation of segmented audiences means the end of that liberal dream. The ambivalence of the term *público* marks an ambivalent critical position. Sarlo is attempting to mark out a new role for the engaged intellectual. Hers is an uncertain but heartfelt faith in the possibility of intellectual engagement: The "door is still ajar" for critical thinking, as she puts it, but no more and no less than ajar.

Note

My thanks to Susan Brook, John King, Alberto Moreiras, and especially Gabriela Nouzeilles for their help with this translation or with this introductory essay.

Bibliography

A much longer bibliography of Beatriz Sarlo's books, articles, and interviews, compiled by Adán Griego, is available online at http://prelectur. stanford.edu/ lecturers/sarlo/biblio.html.

King, John. *Sur: A Study of the Argentine Literary Journal and Its Role in the Development of a Culture, 1931–1970.* Cambridge: Cambridge University Press, 1986.

————. "Las revistas culturales de la dictadura a la democracia: el caso de 'Punto de Vista.'" In *Literatura argentina hoy: de la dictadura a la democracia*. Edited by Karl Kohut and Andrea Pagni, 87–94. Frankfurt: Vervuert Verlag, 1989.

Moreiras, Alberto. "The Order of Order: On the Reluctant Culturalism of Anti-Subalternist Critiques." *Journal of Latin American Cultural Studies* 8.1 (June 1999): 125–45.

Nouzeilles, Gabriela. "The Sense of an Ending: National Community, Liberal Values, and Postmodernity." Unpublished paper, 1999.

Sarlo, Beatriz. *El imperio de los sentimientos: narraciones de circulación periódica en la Argentina 1917–1927*. Buenos Aires: Catálogos, 1985.

————. *Una modernidad periférica: Buenos Aires 1920 y 1930*. Buenos Aires: Nueva Visión, 1988.

————. *La imaginación técnia: sueños modernos de la cultural argentina*. Buenos Aires: Nueva Visión, 1992.

————. *Jorge Luis Borges: A Writer on the Edge*. Edited by John King. London: Verso, 1993.

————. *Instantáneas: medios, ciudad y costumbres al fin de siglo*. Buenos Aires: Ariel, 1996.

————. *La máquina cultural: maestras, traductores y vanguardistas*. Buenos Aires: Ariel, 1998.

————. "Cultural Studies and Literary Criticism at the Crossroads of Values." *Journal of Latin American Cultural Studies* 8.1 (June 1999): 115–24.

Sarlo, Beatriz, and Carlos Altamirano. *Ensayos argentinos: de Sarmiento a la vanguardia*. Buenos Aires: Ariel, 1983.

scenes from

postmodern life

Questions

I could be wrong, but my sense is that public declarations of atheism or, lately, also socialism, produce a certain discomfort. Why not keep to oneself one's convictions concerning such personal matters as God or the social order?
—Roberto Schwarz

Here we are, at the end of the century, in Argentina. A mixture of lights and shadows defines a social landscape that is recognizably part of the Western world. But here the contrasts are extreme, for two reasons: because of our marginality with respect to the "first world" (and as a result, the tributary character of so many processes whose motive force is elsewhere), and because of the callous indifference with which the State entrusts the management of culture to the market, without implementing any policies to offset this development. As is the case with other American nations, Argentina is living out the condition of so-called postmodernity in the paradoxical setting of a nation that is fractured and impoverished. Television is broadcast twenty-four hours daily, on fifty channels, while the school system is in disarray, having to make do without either symbolic prestige or material resources. We have cityscapes whose planning follows the latest design available on the international market, while city services are in a state of crisis. The market in audiovisual goods distributes its trinkets and those who can afford them indulge themselves as if they were living in some wealthy Miami suburb. The very poorest can feed on a diet of "fast-food" television alone. Those who are a little better off have an only slightly greater range of cultural goods from which to choose, as they reflect back on the heyday of the public schools to which they can no longer send their children or from which their children no longer receive what their parents once received. The rich have absolute freedom of choice, as much here as anywhere else.

This inequality scarcely seems to cause any concern. Among those who deny it any importance, there are two major factions, each with its own intellectual cadres. On the one hand, there are the convinced neoliberals, who take no interest in the poor for fear such interest would force public investment that would be hard to translate into the terms of electoral politics or "social peace." On the other hand, there are the market neopopulists, who think that the poor have plenty of innate cultural resources with which to put this "fast-food" television to literally any use. Each faction forgets that old-style populists and old-style liberals alike were never indifferent toward cultural inequality, however much their analyses and proposals for change differed.

Given this intellectual and political climate, it is no surprise that so few concern themselves with an issue the mere mention of which attracts ridicule: the place of art and high culture in the life of society (and, I would add, the place of the humanities within a civilization whose overall tendency is toward technology and science). This topic would appear to be unfashionable, one to be pursued only by university-based specialists or artists themselves, though even they might not always be interested in it. There is no agenda on which the question of art figures not simply for discussion among specialists, but rather as a matter for public intellectual debate.

Yet many are aware that art has been a central issue for the past two hundred years, a period that we are only now leaving behind. Though it is probable that this centrality has faded forever, it is still the case that there is no other human activity that can present us with our condition as subjects and as a society in the way that art does, with such intensity and richness of feeling without the experience demanding, as is the case with religion, that we affirm transcendence. Market neo-populists (whose mode is irony or postmodern disenchant-ment) do away with the issue, treating it as an archaic residue of petit bourgeois moral hang-ups. Like the neoliberals, they put their faith in the market because they think that the market is the place where anyone can be free to choose their Picasso reproduction or their Berlin Philharmonic record, so long as they have the inclination and financial resources. In a world in which almost everyone concurs in diagnosing a "waning of af-fect," it is ironic that this diagnosis does not take into account art as it really is: a practice defined by its production of affect and by its formal and moral intensity.

Argentina is like almost everywhere else in the West in that it is going through a process of increasing cultural homogeniza-tion, whose fundamental trait is, at the same time, an extreme individualism, and in which the wealth of goods on offer is no compensation for the poverty of collective ideals. Evidence for this paradox can be seen in so-called youth culture as it is de-fined by the market, and in a social imaginary possessed by two phantoms: limitless freedom of choice as the abstract affir-mation of individuality, and programmed individualism. The contradictions of this imaginary are the contradictions of *the actually existing postmodern condition*. We see the cloned re-production of needs combined with the fantasy that the satis-faction of these needs is an act of freedom and differentiation. Whereas it has been a characteristic of all societies that they re-produce desires, myths, and habits (because habit is also needed for continuity), our society adds to this the idea that such nor-mative reproduction is in fact an exercise of subjective autono-my. This is the essential paradox that lies behind the cultural homogenization achieved under the banner of absolute free-dom of choice.

Here it seems opportune to pose at least a few questions, even if we know in advance that answers will not simply appear. These questions serve to indicate problems more than they lead to solutions. For in fact the problems we face do not have, and social problems have never had, solutions written into their presentation. We have here questions that will *enable us to see* rather than questions that will uncover, straightaway, a guide to action. The question is not *what is to be done,* but rather *how to set up a standpoint from which we can see.*

If there is any defining feature of intellectual activity today, it would have to be precisely the interrogation of whatever seems written into the nature of things, to *demonstrate that things are not inevitable.* In contrast to the whole gamut of determinisms parading their banners of acceptance and adaptation (technical determinism, market determinism, neopopulist determinism), I wish to counterpose an interrogation whose only pretension would be to upset the justifications, be they celebratory or cynical, of what is. I want to examine the given in the belief that it is a product of social activity whose power is not absolute: *the given is the condition of future action, not its limit.*

Let us take this test to three fields: that of the audiovisual media and their market; that of what were once called popular cultures; and the field of art and "high" culture.

Regarding the first of these: Do we have to accept the way in which the mass media reorganize culture in line with the forms sold to us by a market that operates according to the law of profit and, in our case, without counterweight either from the State or from the public sphere? Are the fates of the market and the audiovisual revolution so closely intertwined that the market is the sole possible agent of audiovisual innovation? Does intervention in the market necessarily imply blocking the development and growth of new cultural forms?

Second: What is the situation of so-called popular cultures at the point at which institutional crisis and audiovisual abundance intersect? What is the circuit whereby spontaneous common sense is made up of a compound of what the media imparts along with traces of older impositions, experiences, and symbolic hardships? What use do popular cultures make of cultural goods from the market? Is it inevitable that popular cultures that are not part of mass media should fall into disarray?

Third: Do we have to resign ourselves to the restricted character of "high" culture? Will art always be (or has it always been) an activity for the leisured, for those with higher callings, or for mandarins? Have we drifted so much that we are now definitively isolated from traditional cultures whose traces are all erased? Is there a place for art in life or do art and life exclude each other in line with some sociological and aesthetic principle?

These questions sketch out a map of hypotheses. They have been formulated in the conviction that the fact that the figure of the intellectual is in disrepute does not mean we should give it a quiet burial, rather that we should learn to avoid the equivocations and the boundless pride that characterized it. It is these equivocations and this pride that lead many to want to bury the intellectual forever, to be done with the intellectual as sovereign legislator or as all-too-lonely prophet. However, past errors do not constitute a sufficient crime to demand our silence. Certainly, intellectuals have no monopoly on the voicing of critique, but there is still moral force in their *obligation toward knowledge.* It is only a matter of a few decades before history will be able to tell whether or not the end of the twentieth century really has seen the critical intellectual's definitive decline.

In the meantime, we are in no hurry to be going.

Chapter 1

Abundance and Poverty

City

In many cities there is no center. By *center* I mean a precise geographic location, marked by monuments and crossroads at which specific streets and avenues intersect, that has theaters, cinemas, restaurants, cafés, pedestrian spaces, and illuminated signs sparkling in the luminous and metallic fluid that bathes the buildings. It may have been arguable whether the center really ended at such and such a street or whether it extended a little farther, but no one would have denied the actual existence of a single center: a place of distinct images and sounds, with its own timetable. A trip to the center from the suburbs was once a special occasion, undertaken on a public holiday, as a night out, a shopping expedition, or, simply, as a chance to see and be in the center. Yet today Los Angeles, that immense decentered city, is not as incomprehensible as it was in the sixties. Many Latin American cities, including Buenos Aires, have embarked upon a process of "Los Angelization."

People today belong more to urban neighborhoods (and to "media neighborhoods") than they did in the twenties, when a trip to the center promised to open up a horizon of desires and dangers, in the exploration of a territory that would always be special. Nobody now leaves middle-class neighborhoods to go to the center. Distances have been cut, not only because the city has stopped growing, but also because people no longer move through the city from one point to another. Richer neighbor-hoods have formed their own centers, which are cleaner, more organized, more secure, and better lit, and which offer more material and symbolic goods.

Going to the center is not the same as going to a shopping center, even if the signifier *center* is repeated in the two expressions. In the first place, the landscape is different. The shopping center or mall, whatever its architectural design, is a scaled-down simulation of a city of services, from which all the extremes of urban experience have been eliminated. The mall eliminates the weather, which was only ever ameliorated rather than eradicated by nineteenth-century passages and arcades. The mall regularizes sound, which never used to be harmonized into any unified program. It softens the play of light and shadow that used to result from the clash of different and opposed light sources contradicting, reinforcing, or simply passing each other by. We no longer experience the huge sense of scale produced by multistory buildings, by cinema or theater frontages two or three stories high, and by glassed surfaces three, four, or five times bigger than the grandest of stores. We no longer see the old familiar monuments whose permanence, beauty, or ugliness made them the most powerful of signs in the urban text. And gone is the proliferation of writing of giant dimensions, once to be found everywhere: on the tops of buildings, stretching for dozens of meters on their facades; on canopies; in huge letters attached to the glass of dozens of entrance and exit doors; or on glittering sheets of metal. There were once coats of arms, placards painted on the lintels of doorways, banners, posters, impromptu signs, printed advertisements, and traffic signposting. All these characteristics, some produced by chance, others by design, are (or were) the mark of urban identity.

Today, and in opposition to this downtown landscape, the mall's project is to construct a space capsule whose structuring aesthetic is that of the market. There is a way in which all shopping centers are the same: in Minneapolis, Miami Beach, Chevy Chase, Newport, or on Rodeo Drive; in Santa Fe or

Coronel Díaz, Buenos Aires. If you were a visitor from Mars, only the currency of the banknotes and the language spoken by merchants, customers, and bystanders could give any indication as to where in the world you were. The constant presence of international brands and merchandise makes for the uniformity of this space without qualities. What we have here is an interplanetary flight to Cacharel, Stephanel, Fiorucci, Kenzo, Guess, and McDonalds, in a spaceship whose insignia is the united colors of the world's labels.

The space capsule can be paradise or nightmare. Air conditioners recycle and clean its air, and the temperature is always mild. The lighting is functional and avoids producing any potentially menacing conflict of light and shadow, while other threats are neutralized by the closed-circuit TV, through which information flows to the panopticon occupied by the security personnel. As in a spaceship, here you can perform all of the activities needed to keep life going: You eat, you drink, you rest, and you consume symbols and merchandise in line with rules that are unwritten but absolutely clear. As in a spaceship, any sense of direction is easily lost: What you see from one position looks so much like what can be seen from any other position that only experts who are familiar with the little details, or people who wander about with map in hand, are able to say where they are at all times. In any case, knowing where you are at each moment loses its importance: You do not make your way through the mall from one point to another as you do in a street or passageway. You have to walk around a mall willing to accept, if not always or completely, the hazards of chance. If you do not accept these hazards, then you are altering the mall's spatial law, its design in which unsought advances, retreats, and repetitions make up a whole sales strategy.

A mall, if it is a good mall, conforms to an overarching order but should at the same time give the idea of freedom of movement. This is the market's ordered drift. If your use of the mall is limited to entering, arriving at a certain point, making a purchase, and leaving straightaway, then you are contradicting the functions of its spatial arrangement, which has much

in common with a Möbius strip: You are to go from one surface to another, from one plane to another without the sensa-
tion of crossing any limit. This arrangement explains precisely
why it is hard to lose your way: The mall is not designed to enable you to arrive at any specific point, and consequently sets
up an unhierarchical space in which it is also hard to tell
whether or not you are lost. The mall is not a labyrinth from
which you would have to look for a way out; far from it, and
comparisons between the mall and a labyrinth are superficial.
The mall is a capsule in which, though you may fail to find
what you are looking for, you will absolutely never get lost.
Only very small children can lose their way in a mall, in that
they may accidentally be separated from other people, and
for them this absence is not redressed by the presence of
merchandise.

Like a spaceship, the mall has an *indifferent* relation to the
city that surrounds it. The city is always the space outside,
whether it takes the form of a highway with a slum at its side, a
grand avenue, a suburb, or a pedestrian space. Inside the mall,
nobody need care whether the store window, through which a
sought-for object is spied, is parallel or perpendicular to a
street outside. At most, what matters is remembering which
little part of the spaceship shelters the desired merchandise.
Alongside the destruction of any sense of orientation within
the mall, the city's geography also disappears completely. Unlike space capsules, malls have their walls sealed off against
any view of outside. More like Las Vegas casinos (and malls
have learned much from Las Vegas), in a mall there is no distinction between day and night. Time does not pass, or at least
what time does pass is also a time without qualities.

For the mall, built to replace the city, the city no longer exists. Hence the mall spares no thought for its surroundings. So
it is not simply that the mall demurely cloisters its precincts off
from any views of the outside; it is more that it constitutes
an invasion, as if it were dropped from the sky upon the city
block that it then brazenly proceeds to ignore. Either that or it
is stuck in the middle of empty ground at the side of a high-

way, in some place with no urban past. When a mall does oc-cupy a space marked by history (as when markets, docks, or port warehouses are converted and recycled, or even in the case of still more cannibalistic recycling, such as with commercial arcades that become arcade malls), this space is put to decorative rather than architectural use. Almost always, and even in the case of "conservationist" malls that keep the older architecture intact, the mall is part and parcel of an evacuation of urban memory, because it represents new customs and does not have to pay tribute to tradition. The wind of novelty makes its force felt wherever the market unfolds.

A mall is all about the future. It builds new habits, by con-verting itself into a point of reference, making the city accom-modate its presence, and familiarizing people with the ways in which they should function in the mall. The mall contains a "premonitory project of the future": There are ever larger malls that, like factory ships, you never have to leave (thus there are already some hotel–spa–cultural center malls in Los Angeles and, of course, Las Vegas). Soon there will be mall-towns, mall-museums, mall-libraries and schools, and mall-hospitals.

We are told that citizenship is formed in the marketplace and that, as a result, malls can be seen as monuments to a new civic sensibility: They are *agora,* combinations of temple and market just like the forum of ancient Rome. The forum had its orators and audiences, its politicians and the plebeians who were the targets of their manipulations. In malls, too, citizens play diverse roles: Some shop, while others simply watch and admire. If in nineteenth-century arcades we find capitalism's archaeology, in malls we see its fullest realization.

By contrast with the real city, which has been built up over time, the mall's version of a small-scale service city comes to us sovereignly independent from tradition or environs. Being a city in miniature, the mall has an air of unreality, because it has been built too quickly, without having to undergo any vac-illation, any progress or delay, any adjustments, destructions, or influences from broader projects. History is absent, and even when there is some mark of historicity, there is none of that impassioned conflict that results when the impulse of the present is set against a resistant past. History is given a sub-servient role and becomes banal decoration, as in the fetishis-tic preservation of a few walls to serve as architectural shell. The mall is therefore perfectly in tune with the decorative pas-sion of so-called postmodern architecture. Purportedly preser-vationist malls treat history paradoxically as souvenir rather than as material support of an identity and a temporality that would always set off some conflict in the present.

Once history has been evacuated to become mere "detail," the mall suffers an amnesia without which the smooth ad-vancement of its business would be impossible. If the traces of history were too evident and went beyond their decorative function, the mall would experience a conflict of functions and meanings: The mall's semiotic machinery has to be that provided by its project alone. By contrast, history abounds with meanings that the mall has no interest in conserving. After all, in the space of the mall it is not meanings that count, but signifiers.

Malls provide perfect evidence for the hypothesis of a con-temporary nomadism: People who have worked their way around a mall once can use any other in a different city, even abroad, without ever having to learn the local language or customs. Temporarily nomadic masses borne on the flows of tourism find in a mall the sweetness of home in that the acci-dents of difference and misunderstanding are erased. After a voyage through unfamiliar cities, the mall is an oasis where everything goes on just as at home. When tourists find them-selves drained by exoticism's delights, they can find peace in the familiarity of spaces that are the same as anywhere else, but whose attractiveness is enhanced by the knowledge that they are "abroad." Without malls and without Club Meds, mass tourism would be unthinkable: Both provide the security felt only in your own house without completely losing the emotion produced by the fact of leaving home behind. When a foreign space, in its sheer resistance to communication, is as threaten-ing as a desert, the mall offers the palliative of familiarity.

But this familiarity is not the only or even the most important of the mall's contributions to nomadism. On the contrary, the mall as a perfect machine that operates according to fuzzy logic is itself a playing field for deterritorialized drift. Its points of reference are universal: Its logos, acronyms, texts, and manners do not require their interpreters to be settled in any culture previous to or distinct from that of the market. Thus the mall produces an extraterritorial culture from which nobody can feel excluded. Even petty consumers manage perfectly in the mall, inventing various unforeseen uses for it that the machine tolerates to the extent that these uses do not divert the energies that the mall administers. In the richer parts of town I have seen women from the suburbs sitting on the sides of flower tubs, right next to the overflowing tables of a food court, feeding their babies while other children run among the counters with a two-liter plastic bottle of Coca-Cola. I have seen them take homemade sandwiches from plastic bags marked with international brands, bags that no doubt have been successively recycled from the moment they left the stores, fulfilling the laws of a first "legitimate" use. The mall machine did not foresee these visitors, though it does not actively expel them; they are extraterritorial, and yet the extraterritoriality of the mall itself allows them a curiously paradoxical plebeian liberty. Faithful to the market's universality, the mall operates according to a principle of nonexclusivity.

This extraterritoriality offers advantages for the poorest members of society, who lack a city that is clean and safe, with good services, where they can walk around at any time of day. The poor live in suburbs from which the State has retreated, and where poverty prevents the market from taking the State's place. They bear the brunt of the crisis of local neighborhoods, the deterioration of community solidarities, and violence's anecdotal everydayness. Malls are precisely an exaggerated and condensed realization of qualities opposed to these traits of urban poverty. Moreover, entering this extraterritorial space requires no special visas. For the other end of the social spectrum, the mall's extraterritoriality could infringe upon what middle and upper strata of society consider to be their rights, yet the mall's timetabled and stratified patterns of use prevent the collision of these two distinct claims upon it. The poor go there on the weekend, when the slightly better off and the rich prefer to be elsewhere. One and the same space changes according to the day and time, demonstrating that transsocial quality that some consider to be the hallmark of postmodernity.

The mall's extraterritoriality also fascinates the very young, precisely because of the possibility it gives of drifting through the world of mercantile signifiers. The mall displays the richest of scenographies for brand-name fetishism. Here, at least in theory, there is no lack; on the contrary, malls need excess to an extent that surprises even the most erudite of cognoscenti. This scenography reveals the mall's Disney World face: As in Disney World, all your favorite characters are there, all of them showing off what made them famous. The mall is an exhibition of all the objects of your dreams.

This space without urban references is instead full of "neocultural" references, which allow the uninitiated to learn a kind of "know-how" acquired just by being there. The market, in empowering freedom of choice (however much this may only be an imaginary taking of sides), provides an education in subjects that are functional for its own dynamic, while also suiting young people's desire to be free from institutions. Adolescents know more about malls than anyone else does, and they can apply an antisentimental sentimentality in their enthusiasm for the exhibitionism and freedom of movement that controlled disorder promotes. The brands and labels that make up the mall landscape replace the array of public or religious symbols now entering into decline. Moreover, for kids caught by the "high-tech" bug of computers, malls offer a space that seems "high tech" however much, in its suburban exemplars, this may be an aesthetic effect rather than a real functional quality. Furthermore, malls combine the iconographic fullness of their amassed brand names with the "artesanal" brands of some folk-ecological-natural products, thus making for the sum of styles that defines an adolescent aesthetic: industrial kitsch meets compact disc.

The speed with which malls have imposed themselves upon urban culture makes this a change in our customs unlike any other, even in this century so marked by the vagaries of the market and shifting values. It may be argued that this change is superficial and cannot be compared to other social upheavals, but I believe that it synthesizes basic characteristics of what is to come or, rather, of what is already here to stay. In cities that are coming apart and breaking down, this refuge against atomization is perfectly suited to the mood of an epoch. Where institutions and the public sphere can no longer construct landmarks that are considered eternal, a monument has arisen whose premise is precisely the speed of commercial flow. Malls hold up a mirror that reflects a crisis of public space in which it is difficult to construct meanings; and the reflected image is an inverted one, in which an ordered torrent of signifiers flows day and night.

Market

The following conversation was overheard a little while ago, on a Sunday midafternoon, in an emptying restaurant. The girl's parents were asking her what she wanted for her birthday.

"You know already," the girl said. "The operation you promised me last year, on my fourteenth birthday."

Hoping to change her mind, they offered her instead a month on a Caribbean beach; skiing holidays for her and a friend; private lessons in aerobic skating or hang gliding; running shoes either with a tachometer or a built-in pump, or in an older style with a thin sole trimmed with satin and lined with synthetic sable perfect for après-ski; permission for her boyfriend to sleep over every night; an original Calvin Klein party dress; a superlight compact disc player she could carry in her purse; a life-size inflatable Axl Rose doll; a life-size inflatable Luis Miguel doll; a passive exercise bed and solarium; contact lenses in green, steel gray, and turquoise; a life-size hologram of her head; a mural for her room of the first photograph taken of her after her birth; a haircut; permanent eyeliner and dyed eyebrows; a party at the nightclub of her choosing; a giant Sarah Kay bear.

"I want the operation," the girl insisted.

"I think your hips are developed just fine for your age," her mother reasoned.

"I don't like my bottom," the girl said with certainty.

"I don't see anything special about it," said her little brother.

"Exactly," she said stubbornly.

"You're still too young to decide," said the father.

"All my friends have had something done or are going to do something to celebrate their fifteenth birthday, and I don't want to be the stupid one left behind."

"What's stupid is having the operation," said the little brother, "seeing how much it must hurt."

"Nobody understands me," said the girl.

Her father became serious: "We understand you perfectly; nobody should be denied their rights, but it will end up being very expensive."

"It will turn out being even more expensive when nobody loves me, when nobody takes my photo on the beach, and when I don't appear in the magazines. That'll be expensive, the amount wasted on therapy and the fact that I won't be able to work at anything when I'm older."

"She has something there," said her mother.

"There was never any question about how much your face-lift cost," the girl said, not realizing she had no need to attack her allies.

"I paid for my facelift; I went to the clinic with a purse full of notes and still there was money to spare."

"Who knows where you took it from," the girl said.

"Money doesn't smell," said her little brother.

"I took the money from the study," said the mother.

"From whose study?" asked the brother.

"Idiot, this boy is an idiot," said the father.

"The way I am, with this flat bottom, I'm ashamed even of going to school. All the girls have had something done: nose jobs, cheekbones raised, lower lips enlarged, forehead-minimizing hair implants, chintucks, breast implants, breasts reshaped, pubic-hair electrolysis, lower ribs sawn off, hips seen to, bottoms raised, toes straightened, insteps lifted, wrists reduced, pectoral muscle implants, arms reshaped, bones lengthened, necks stretched, skin peels with natural acids. And what if I were asking for hair implants? That's much worse, because you don't know if you're going to keep using them. That really is throwing money away, like on this moron's tattoos."

"Leave me out of it," her little brother shot back.

"We're not millionaires," said her mother.

"What's that got to do with my present? Since I've started high school you've had the bags under your eyes removed, a nose job, two collagen injections, and an operation on your belly so you could return to a size two. How many birthdays have you had since I started high school? Three. How many operations have you had?"

"But they weren't under general anesthetic, and in any case you two were to blame for the belly."

"Leave me out of it," said the little brother.

"OK," said the father, "but don't ask for anything else until you're eighteen."

"By eighteen I'll be a millionaire living in Miami," said the girl.

Later, her mother mentioned that she would have a couple more touch-ups before anyone noticed her eyelids were drooping a little. "At two touch-ups a year, if I live till I'm seventy-five that's around sixty touch-ups, but you never know what will come up along the way."

The person who really needed an operation was the father. With those bags under his eyes, if he were fired he wouldn't be able to find a decent job anywhere. "This year I'll have an operation too," the father said. "When all's said and done more depends on me than on all of you put together."

We are free. At every step we will be still freer to redesign our bodies. Today it is surgery, tomorrow it will be genetics, and all our dreams come or will come true once more. Whose dreams are these? It is our culture dreaming, and we are the products of our cultural icons' dreams. We allow ourselves into the dreams of magazine covers, billboards, advertising, and fashion. Each of us lights on a thread promising to lead us to something profoundly personal in the tapestry woven with our absolutely shared desires. This home of dreams, where we can organize fragments from all over to construct the "language of our social identity," compensates for modern society's instability. In our culture's dreams we are part of a patchwork of fragments, a collage of different elements, an always unfinished ensemble of everything, each piece marked by the year that it was cut to shape, the place that it came from, and the original that it tries to imitate.

It is said that identities have been exploded. In their place we see not a vacuum, but the market. The social sciences find that citizenship is also exercised in the market, and that those who cannot carry out their transactions there are left, so to speak, off the edge of the world. Fragments of subjectivity are picked up in this planetary scene of circulation from which the poorest are excluded. The market unifies, selects, and, moreover, produces the illusion of difference through the extra-mercantile meanings taken on by objects acquired through mercantile exchange. The market is a linguistic system and we all try to speak one or more of its dialects: Our dreams have all too little to play with. Our dreams are made up of bits and pieces found in the market. Centuries ago such bits and pieces had other sources, not necessarily any better. The critique of these dreams was an important motivation for constructing images of alternative societies. Today, then, critique should take as its object the serial dreams of the market.

Desire for the new is by definition inextinguishable. The aesthetic avant-gardes learned something of this desire, in that once the floodgates of tradition, religion, and indisputable authority break open, then the *perpetuum mobile* of the new becomes the operative principle. This principle of perpetual innovation also holds true for the market; indeed, it is truer for the market than for any other sphere.

These days, the subject in a position to enter the market,

with enough money to participate as a consumer, is a type of *collector in reverse*. Instead of collecting the things themselves, she collects the acts of acquiring things. Collectors of the old type take things out of circulation and use in order to hoard them: No stamp collector would send a letter using the stamps from a collection; no connoisseur of lead soldiers would let a child play with them; matchboxes in a collection are not to be used. Traditional collectors know the market value of their possessions (because they have paid for them); or they know the time and labor that has been invested in getting hold of them, if the collection has not been built through sale and purchase. But collectors also know what we could call the syntactic value that these items have as a collection: They know what they need to complete a set, what they would not swap for anything else, and the history behind each individual item. In a traditional collection, valuable items are literally irreplaceable, even if a collector might sacrifice one item to obtain another that is even more valuable.

Collectors in reverse, on the other hand, know that the items they acquire lose value from the moment they come into their hands. An object's value begins to erode, and the force of attraction that once made things shine in the market showplace fades. Once acquired, merchandise loses its soul (whereas in a collection, by contrast, things have a soul that becomes richer the more the collection is enriched: Collections give value to old age). No object could be adequate to the desire of the collector in reverse, because there will always be another object of attraction. What are collected are acts of sale and purchase—perfectly incandescent, glorious moments. North Americans, who know something of these vicissitudes of modernity and postmodernity, give the name *shopping spree* to a type of purchasing orgy in which one thing leads to another until exhaustion brings the day to a close in the department store café. In theory, the shopping spree is an impulse that cannot be held back so long as there are still the economic means to keep going. It is precisely a collection of acts of consumption in which the object is consumed before it is even touched by use.

At the opposite pole from collectors in reverse are those excluded from the market, who range from those who can at any rate dream of imaginary consumption to those so excluded that poverty pens them in, confining them to the most minimal of fantasies. These people wear things out through consumption; acquisition alone does not make them lose interest, as they see using an object as a fundamental dimension of its possession. But leaving aside the case of these people who have not been invited to the party, nowadays the desire for things is almost inextinguishable for those who have understood the game and are in a position to play it.

Material objects escape us. At times because we cannot grasp them, at times because we already have them in our grasp, but they always escape us. Identity's impermanence affects collectors in reverse as much as it does the less favored imaginary collectors: Both think that material objects compensate (or would compensate) for some lack. In each case, this lack that is to be filled exists not so much at the level of possession, but rather at the level of identity. Thus objects signify *us*: There are meanings they can grant us, and these are meanings we are ready to accept. A traditionalist would say that this is a case of a world turned completely upside down. But when religion, ideology, politics, the traditional bonds of community, and modern social relations all fail to offer any foundation for the construction of identity or any adequate ground for value, then the market steps in to provide a space of universal freedom, giving us something to replace the gods that failed. Material objects become our icons when the symbolic power of other icons, which used to represent some divinity, is seen to wane; they are our icons because they can create an imagined community, a community of consumers, whose sacred book is advertising, whose ritual is the shopping spree, whose temple is the mall, and whose law is fashion.

Still, objects escape us, and it is not just those who cannot enter the market with confidence, or those who cannot even take part, who find that objects elude their desire. The same quality that makes material objects desirable also makes them volatile. Their instability finds its source precisely in the sacred book of advertising and in the knowledges codified each season in the encyclopedia of fashion. Material objects gain their value because they change constantly; paradoxically, they also lose their value because they change constantly. They stop being part of the fabric of life. None of us would want to use a pair of old sneakers just because we had once been happy wearing them. Sometimes sentimentalism can save things from disappearing: We keep football shirts, a wedding dress, or our first school uniform. So sentimentalism is a psychological form of collectionism. But in general, the passing of time leaves no sign of distinction, simply the signs of age, and old objects have no defenders equivalent to the conservationists who plead for cities or buildings. Only things in the public domain call for preservation. In the private sphere, objects age rapidly, and only perfect design could save them from this aging process. But not even perfect design can truly save them, as objects that have been designed perfectly end up in museums or collections, while objects of "common" design (generally those that particularly bear the signs that they were once in fashion) are only kept when they cannot be replaced by other, newer and better, objects.

Time has been abolished when it comes to the market's everyday objects, not because they are eternal but rather because they are *completely transitory*. They last only so long as their symbolic value does not completely wear off because, in addition to being commodities, they are also hypersignifying objects. In the past, only objects of (civil or religious) worship or works of art had this ability to add to their use value a surplus value of meaning that made them more significant. Today this is true of the market, as much as it is of religion or power. The market gives material objects a symbolic surplus that is fleeting but is as powerful as any other symbol. Things give rise to a meaning that goes beyond utility or beauty, or rather their utility or beauty are byproducts of a meaningfulness derived from the hierarchy of the market. It is not just a matter of chance that material objects at the center and summit of this hierarchy are more beautiful (better designed) than those that form the base or the intermediate levels of the pyramid. It is true that the market is not just some ship of fools that judges excellence on the basis of a label without taking notice of a thing's qualities. Nevertheless, the perceived excellence of a brand, a label, or a signature always has some other foundation beyond its material qualities, its functionality, or its design perfection.

All this is common knowledge. Yet material objects keep on escaping us. They have become so valuable for the construction of identity, so central to the discourse of fantasy, and they stigmatize so terribly those who do not have them, that they seem to be made of the same resistant and intangible material as dreams. In the face of an unstable, fragmentary reality that undergoes processes of the most rapid metamorphoses, material objects are an anchor, albeit a paradoxical anchor that itself has to change with time, to rust and decay, becoming obsolescent the day of its first use. The power of objects is built on these paradoxes. Likewise, the freedom of those who consume them arises out of the market's ironclad need to turn us into permanent consumers. Our materialist dreams are free, but it is the most powerful of persuaders that has the ear of this freedom and speaks to us through it.

The world of material objects has grown and will keep growing. Up until a few decades ago, commodities had an external materiality and only exceptionally did they enter into the intimacy of our bodies. Nowadays, the market is like an inexorably rising tide, flooding every territory imaginable. We dream of things that will alter our bodies, and this is the happiest and most terrifying of dreams. Desire, which has yet to find itself calmed even temporarily by any material object, has found in the objectification of the body itself the ne plus ultra to unite the myths of beauty and youth. A race against time is on, and the market proposes the consoling fiction that age can be deferred and perhaps, if not today then maybe tomorrow, defeated forever.

If the indignity surrounding commodities' aging has removed temporality from our daily life (the time of material objects only counts for those who cannot replace them with other, newer ones), now we are offered objects that change our bodies. Prostheses, synthetics, and artificial aids are introduced into the body through operations that modify it according to design standards that vary every five years (who now wants the flat chests that were the vogue ten years ago, or the daintiness of the sixties?). When on public display, bodies should be perfectly functional and resistant to age, as was once expected of commodities. There is no reason to reject this surgical technology, and so to reprise the scandalized reaction of decent nineteenth-century women who refrained from dyeing their hair. It is not a question of being horrified today by operations that in ten years' time we ourselves will consider innocent. We have to question, however, what it is that society is searching for in these transformations produced by corporeal engineering or market design.

Who is it that speaks as we dream of beauty? What will happen to us if we manage not only to prolong life, but also, to put it simply, to abolish death?

Youth

There is much to say about costume, and the art of disguise. At nightclubs, in the early hours of the morning, the young enact their own form of ceremony. Here is the carnival that we all once thought had disappeared from urban culture for good. Yet the end of the century unearths it again, dressed up to go out at night.

Let there be no confusion: The girl over there who looks like a prostitute from the pages of a Spanish *movida* or "new wave" cartoon, is simply wearing a mask. She is disguised as a prostitute, but it would be a complete misunderstanding to confuse her with a real prostitute (who, by contrast, would not be done up like her, but would be dressed to look like a model). To confuse her with a prostitute would be like going to a carnival in the 1920s and making the mistake of believing that the "old dame" or the "Russian ballerina" had in fact come from the eighteenth century or was indeed Russian. The girl over there has made up her face and has adorned her body with a series of signs that no longer signify what they used to: Her transparent black blouse is not a transparent black blouse; the purple lips are not purple lips; the almost-bared breasts are not bared breasts; nor are the military boots, military boots; and the uncompromising miniskirt, right up to her thighs and pubis, is not a miniskirt. The girl has picked a mask for use in the small hours. This is not some version of her mother's party dress, nor the outcome of a negotiation between a princess's outfit and her family's economic possibilities. Her style of dress owes nothing to any fashion except that set by the tastes of teenage nightclubs; this style is nothing like that of the young women of the fifties whose aim when they dressed to drink tea at a boîte would have been to be kitsch copies of their mothers or of ladies they had seen in films. Like her male friend (with his T-shirt painted in more or less Rasta colors, the tattoo on his biceps, and his earrings) the girl over there is wearing a costume specific to the nightclub, a disguise on whose terrain humor and eroticism collide.

The carnival's pure exteriority produces an effect of superficiality, in which everything is completely on view. Here fashion sets out to denude, breaking away from its traditional function of oscillating between the seen and the unseen. Dressing up to party is the apotheosis of insinuation, as the nightclub disguise almost completely achieves an ideal of total visibility. In dressing up to party, there can be no compromise with anything outside the chosen outfit's semantic system: Shoes, purse, jewels, and perfume all have to be part of whatever it is that the outfit signifies. The costume gains life from a certain discontinuity, and its surprising beauty comes from the art of the unforeseen, from a combinatorial fantasy more than from the canon. Like hippie clothing of the sixties, nightclub costume does not shrink from combining differing temporalities and origins: retropunk, retroromantic, retrocabaret, retrofolk, retromilitary, retro–Titanes in the Ring, retro-Rasta, gigolo, femme fatale, demimondaine, or Almodóvar prostitute. As in carnivalesque disguise (which Madonna reproduces with deliberate faithfulness), the prefix *retro* is a basic trait of a style based more in recycling than in the production of the totally new. Its originality is syntactic, evoking collage and not refusing the strategy of the "ready-made."

The girl's dress mixes two temporal points of reference. There is a counterpoint between the body and its costume. The clothes are not chosen to flatter the body, which would be in line with an easy calculus that has historically only allowed certain liberties to certain bodies—the more perfect the body, the freer the choice of fashion to cover it. On the contrary, the girl first chooses her costume and only then layers, swathes, and drapes it on a body that has to adapt to the costume because the costume is more important than the body, even though the body is freely on display. The girl's choice is not based upon thinking through what suits her best. Instead, she has put on the costume that she likes best or, simply, the one she ought to wear. The idea of carnival takes precedence over other ideas, and in the carnival what flatters bodily beauty has to give way to the imperative that bodies should come out transfigured by costume. There are things that can be seen only in a nightclub; a party dress, on the other hand, could be worn to the theater or at a wedding.

In the old days, stars of popular culture never used to dress differently when they gave a concert. For Doris Day or Bing Crosby, only a surplus charge of glamour, rather than any particular outfit, set them apart from conventional Western fashion as decreed by the catwalks or in magazines. When Gardel dressed as a gaucho or Maurice Chevalier wore his boulevardier outfit of straw hat and bowtie, it was still clear that this was just decorative excess that could not and would not be taken any further, beyond the stage.

Since the sixties, by contrast, rock culture has turned dress into a central feature of style. Rock was always more than a musical genre, and from the outset it was animated by the pulse of a counterculture whose effects would be felt even in everyday life. Rock's identity was extramusical: Sustained by the music, rock culture staked out a terrain of mobilization, resistance, and experimentation. Drugs, which had been part of the private habits of curious members of the bourgeoisie, of decadent poets, dandies, and those who wished to explore subjectivity, became part of rock culture. Within rock culture, drug use became a mixture of public assertion and a limit that had to be crossed. Even today, the collective imagination makes a moralistic and invidious association between young people and drugs. Rock was a form of defiance for the young (perhaps the last such), and those who pointed to its subversive potential founded on the emergence of libertarian ideologies were right. Rock's rebelliousness heralded a spirit of contestation that was part and parcel of the movement that saw waves of young people entering the political scene at the end of the sixties. The protagonists in rock and in politics may not have been the same, but even if they were different, even when they took no notice of each other, they were part of the same cultural climate.

Rock has fulfilled one of its possible destinies: No longer program, it has become style. Rock's delayed expansion into less rebellious youth culture comes complete with the recycling of romantic, Satanic, and exceptionalist myths. As style, it presents itself as a resource for the market, which takes up rock's founding fathers to underline their pop elements. Moreover, this process of assimilation is not new; it has been part of the script as one way in which rock circulated from its beginning. Brothers and enemies, rock and pop traveled along intersecting paths even when rock's aesthetic quality was at its highest. So rock has become a resource available for anyone to plunder. It has become just one stratum of modern culture, its subversive aspects erased with the death of its heroes or now that the survivors from the old days are taking up more pietistic discourses (turning to ecology, naturalism, spirituality, or New Age beliefs).

Become style (and the same thing happened to the historic avant-gardes), rock is now cited by every strain of youth culture. If rock, like the hippies, found in dress a mark of exceptionality, nowadays the idea of dress as a means of differentiation between cultural tribes has spread everywhere, in all sorts of permutations. Style indicators come and go, as black windjammers return for a season, punk's lights and shadows might be the rage in cosmetics, skinhead outrages are recycled in tattoos, leather displaces jeans, jeans displace leather, Brylcremed DAs replace shaved necks, and kids who are no doubt racist at heart dress in Bob Marley T-shirts. Dress comes to attract attention through its boisterously obsolescent splendor and its sovereign arbitrariness.

So the girl in the nightclub testifies to a form of amnesia. She pays no heed to the origin of the styles that mesh on her body. Her costume has no past (just as "Russian ballerina" dress signified neither folkloric dance nor Russian nationality), and it is not the semantic meaning of the elements brought together that differentiates her, but their syntactic articulation. Her costume is pure form, and it distinguishes itself from "legitimate" fashion form in that it aspires not to universality but rather to a particular social subset. It is a mark of her age and her status as a youth, rather than of her social or financial status. The girl and her costume bring to fruition and take us back to something whose outline could already be seen in the fifties: This is "youth style." Youth here is not a category that refers to age; it is an aesthetic of everyday life.

Childhood has almost disappeared, pushed out by an increasingly early adolescence. Youth is prolonged until thirty. A third of life is spent under the heading of youth, a heading as conventional as any other. Everyone knows that these boundaries, though taken to be precise markers, have changed over time.

In 1900 an immigrant woman who already had two children would not have been thought *particularly* young at sixteen, and her husband, ten years older, would have been fully an adult. In the past, the poor were hardly ever young people, and the nature of their world meant that they passed from childhood to the culture of work without any transitional stage. Those who did not follow this itinerary were classified as dangerous exceptions: They were juvenile delinquents, their photographs making them look like little adults, producing a similar effect as photographs of stunted children. Here youth was regarded not so much as a source of value than as a sign of danger (a habit of thinking shed by criminology but maintained by the police to the present day).

Yet in 1918, students in Córdoba, Argentina, initiated a movement for university reform, formulating their demands on behalf of young people. Latin American intellectuals in the first decades of the twentieth century, such as José Ingenieros, José Enrique Rodó, Alfredo Palacios, and Víctor Raúl Haya de la Torre, believed that they were speaking for the young, and they found that instituting a dialogue with the young could profit those who wished to set themselves up as their mentors. The leaders of the Cuban revolution and those who marched through Paris in May 1968 also identified themselves as young people. Yet the leaders of the 1917 Russian Revolution, at the same age, had not been young: Revolutionary youth at the beginning of the century believed that they had to fulfill obligations rather than demand special rights. Their messianism was that of the Latin American guerrillas in that it valorized a moral tone or political imperative that required the young to act as historical actors who would be more daring, free from all traditional ties.

By contrast, earlier the Romantics found youth to make an aesthetic and political argument. Rimbaud, at the cost of silence and exile, invented the modern myth of youth as transsexual, innocent, and perverse. The Argentine avant-gardes of the twenties practiced a style of intervention later judged juvenile; by contrast, Bertolt Brecht was never young, nor were Walter Benjamin, Theodor Adorno, or Roland Barthes. Photographs of Sartre, Raymond Aron, and Simone de Beauvoir when they were barely twenty years old give off a posed gravity, with which those pictured hoped to dispel any notion of that immaturity that so fascinated Gombrowicz. We were young, said Nizan, but let nobody tell me that the twenties are the time of your life. David Viñas was not *particularly* young ce and Poverty 31

when, at twenty-seven, he edited the jou_ _Contorno, in_
which the category of "youth" was stigmat. _Juan José_
Sebreli, himself two or three years younger th_as; when_
they talked of a "new generation" they used thi_o mark_
an ideological difference that would be quite co_with-_
out any resort to a vindication of youth.

Orson Welles was not *all that* young when h_
Citizen Kane at twenty-four. Luis Buñuel, Alfred H_
and Ingmar Bergman never made any "young cinema_
way that Jim Jarmusch or Jean-Luc Godard have done._
Garbo, Louise Brooks, Ingrid Bergman, and María Félix _
never teenagers; even when they were *very* young, they alw_
appeared to be *only* young people. Audrey Hepburn was th_
first teenager in American cinema: Only child prodigies were
younger. Frank Sinatra and Miles Davis were never young in
the way that the Beatles were. Even Elvis Presley did not stage
his youth as his most valuable asset, in that although he ap-
pealed strongly to teenagers, his subversion had more to do
with sexuality than with youth. Jimi Hendrix never seemed to
be as young as that eternal youth, the aged youth and frozen
teenager, Mick Jagger.

Before jeans and miniskirts, there was no such thing as
youth fashion, nor was there a market in which it could circulate. Mary Quant, Lee, and Levi's constitute the academy for
this new design. Up until 1960, the young imitated, stylized or,
at most, parodied what was, simply, fashion. So photos of
younger actors, football players, or university students before
this time fail to evoke the now commonplace iconography of
perverse altar boys or rockers ready for anything. This iconography is only a quarter of a century old. Models in advertising
used to imitate actresses or the upper class; now models imitate
younger models, and actresses imitate models. It is only with
men that maturity retains some sexual magnetism. Madonna
provides an original challenge because she takes on retro fashion without incorporating the elements of youth style. She
originated a form of costume or disguise, worn only by the
young, that complicates the meanings of teenage brands that

~together to make up a fashion that displays
are here bro~ that have built up over the past half century.
the stylisti~

~ has more prestige than ever, in a manner that be-
Tod~ ~s whose hierarchical principles have been destabi-
~ildhood no longer adequately sustains illusions of
~ess, of the pacifying suspension of sexuality and inno-
~. The category of "youth," on the other hand, guarantees
~ther *set of illusions,* with the advantage that sexuality can
~e summoned onto the scene and at the same time be deployed
freer of its adult obligations, among which is a black-and-
white definition of sex. So we all want to dwell indefinitely in
this territory constituted by youth. But the "young" expel all
phonies from this territory, casting out those who do not fulfill
the conditions of age; they then engage in a generational war
made banal by cosmetics, by the unending cycle of cosmetic
surgery every five years, and by "New Age" therapies.

Youth culture, universal and tribal at the same time, is constructed in the context of an institution, traditionally dedicated
to the young, that is now in crisis. This is the school, whose
prestige has been weakened as much by the breakdown of traditional authorities as by the conversion of the mass media
into a space of symbolic abundance that the schools cannot
match. With this breakdown in authority, the strategies once
employed to define what is allowed and what is forbidden are
in crisis. Permanence, once authority's constitutive trait, is cut
short by the flux of novelty. When it is almost impossible to
define what is allowed and what is forbidden, morality ceases
being a terrain of significant conflicts, to become a catalogue
of banal statements. Authority has lost its terrible and intimi-
dating aspect (which stirred rebellion) and is now only authority when it exercises (as it does with increasing frequency)
repressive force. Whereas before, prohibition relied upon discourse and could therefore be confronted, now it seems that
only the police remain. What was a few decades ago the site of
politics is where, first, social movements appeared, and, now,
a fleet of neoreligions gains ground.

The market takes up the baton dropped... and Poverty
courts the youth it has instituted as protago... uthority, and
myths. One could plot a graph on which the r... most of its
influence of the market and the declining weigh... gemonic
would be seen to cross, and this would be a goo... chool
resent a more general tendency. The young grad... ep-
role as characters within a novel of domesticity that...
an ever briefer childhood, and move to the hyperrea...
opera that stages commodities dancing both for those v...
afford to buy them as well as for the other consumers...
only resource is their imagination. For those "imaginary...
sumers," the new poor, the vision of a life of labor and sa...
fice is not such an effective interpellation as it was for the
grandparents, among other reasons because it will not even
give them what it gave their grandparents, or because they do
not want to achieve merely what their grandparents sought.

Whether they be consumers in fact or consumers in imagination, the young discover in the market of commodities and symbolic goods a depository of material objects and hot-off-the-shelf discourses prepared specially for them. The speed of market circulation and its associated accelerated obsolescence combine to form an allegory of youth: In the market, commodities have to be new, have to be fashionably in style, and have to be in tune with the most insignificant changes that are in the air at the time. The incessant renovation needed by the capitalist market captures the myth of permanent novelty that also motivates youth. Never have the needs of the market been so precisely calibrated to its consumers' imaginary as they are today.

The market has two faces: It promises both a form of ideal freedom as well as guaranteed exclusion. Just as racism reveals itself at the doors of certain nightclubs whose bouncers are experts in social differentiations, so the market chooses those who are to be in a position to choose within it. Yet because it has to be universal, the market articulates its discourse as though everyone were equal. The mass media reinforce this idea of equality in liberty that makes up a central part of well-meaning

youth idea s. In these ideologies, real inequalities are ignored to equip a culture that is stratified but at the
sam tterned by the magnetic poles of musical identity
'strata e sites at which identity itself is experienced. It is
ed symbolically underside, at society's margins, that this conglomera-
n of a continuity strata shows its cracks. In any case, the cracks are
nces are disguised ed symbolically, as videos and pop music create the illu-
n of a continuity within which socially determined differ-
nces are disguised as individual choices. If it is true, as has
been said, that idolizing a pop star involves the same kind of
love as following a football team, these affects' transclass character pacifies their bearers' consciences. Their consciences suitably pacified, these same people will go on to take a certain
snobbish pleasure in making careful distinctions between
sheep and goats in line with the same classificatory logic that is
found at the nightclub doors. The egalitarian impulse sometimes believed to be found in youth culture reaches its limits in
social, racial, sexual, and moral prejudice.

The fact that young people's ties to any community of values
are so weak finds its compensation in a more abstract but
equally powerful arrangement: A bright and unruffled imaginary picks up on themes that will ensure that, precisely, youth
itself is the source of the values through which this same imaginary interpellates the young. The circle is almost perfectly
closed.

Video Games

I enter a place that combines the sound of a nightclub with the
lighting of a dockside bar. Its patrons look variously as though
they have come straight from high school, from a slum, or
from offices where they work at the lowest grade of specialization and salary. They are each absorbed in what they are doing,
and their eyes never meet. From time to time one or another of
them will walk to the counter at the back and make a transac-
tion; whoever it is serving them distrusts his clients, preferring
to maintain only the most indispensable of contacts. I am the

only woman in the place. Later, two girls enter who appear to be friends of one of the students.

The room's walls are painted in psychedelic colors, apple green, yellow, and violet; the light coming from spotlights hung from the ceiling bounces off these planes of color, and there are also some shimmering neon signs, rays, stars, and spirals. But who cares, because no one looks at either the walls or floor; no one has time to look around. They know that there is little to see. The sound of the music, a repetitive beat with few variations overlaid by the briefest of simple melodies that also repeats itself without variations, mixes with another series of sounds: whistles, metallic shocks, deafening crashes, brief waves of electronic sound, rattles, synthesizer chords, gunshot sounds, indecipherable voices, boing, bang, and clash, all sounding like a cartoon soundtrack.

The ceiling spotlights compete with other sources of light: glints, rays, abrupt illuminations, total blackouts, varying planes of color, and halos that reflect on walls and bodies. These are light effects that draw attention to themselves, whose value lies in what they are and not in what they make visible around them. These light effects are like things in themselves, filling the place and converting it into a hologram. Without the light and sound, the place would be empty, because the truth is that these effects are its furniture. This is a light scene in which each square yard offers a clearly delimited arrangement of color and sound, which enables each person to stay self-absorbed in his or her own space.

If I take up a position near one of the patrons, a little to one side, so that I can see what he is doing, he does not divert his gaze, and this lack of contact lets me assume I am not too much of a nuisance. His eyes are preoccupied with a video screen, his hands apart, deftly operating the joysticks and buttons of a control panel. Occasionally a movement of the head lets me suppose some surprise, contradiction, or happiness, but in general these are hardly demonstrative people. They are absorbed and preoccupied by the visual arrangement of the screen as it changes, registering the immediate results of their actions or the inscrutable decisions of the computer chips.

Every three, four, or five minutes it starts all over again. Some letters appear on the screen to show that even if everything seems to go on the same forever, in fact the counter is back at zero and you have to begin building your score up from scratch. The machines constitute an *infinite recurrence*, every so often finishing a cycle and starting up another that is basically identical, but that is at the same time characterized by its variations. Like an infinite recurrence, these variations hypnotically coax you to aim for an unreachable limit, beyond which a player would beat the machine.

On the other side of the room is a more archaic world. Vertical and horizontal panels, kitted out in the pop aesthetic of fifties' graphic art, offer surfaces covered with obstacles (mushrooms, bridges, pits, rails, mazes, and arches), around which runs a metal ball, advancing, retreating, and disappearing. It advances, retreats, and disappears, but in doing so it makes music, the music played by the player with her hands by the sides of the horizontal panel, who is preventing the sphere from falling into the well in which it will be stuck until everything goes back to the beginning once again. I notice that the players bang and tilt the machine, pushing its legs and sides, controlling it with all their bodies, not just with their hands alone. Various parts of the vertical panel are lit up, to show pictures of animals, midgets, roulette wheels, spaceships, gorillas, jungles, beaches, swimming pools, women, soldiers, dinosaurs, and athletes. These pictures are real pictures, unlike the geometric figures on most of the screens, and the sounds also have an air of reality in that the sphere in motion physically hits against the mushrooms or the metal rails.

These machines (the ones without screens) are reminiscent of a casino: Las Vegas in a six-by-three-foot space. I mean more than just that the casinos of Las Vegas are full of machines like this, and of screens like those lining the opposite wall; rather I mean that each of these machines combines the sounds and lights, the repetition, concentration, and infinite recurrence of a casino. What is more, they copy the Las Vegas aesthetic (or perhaps it would be better to say that Las Vegas and these machines share the same aesthetic).

I retrace my steps and come to the exit. On either side of the door are two huge screens showing a ball game. Just like on television, here the score appears at the bottom of the screen, identifying the teams by the color of their shirts. After watching a slice of this truly infinite and recurrent match, a man next to me goes to the counter and returns with a token, all set to intervene and change the machinic order of things.

In other places like this one I have seen at the back something like a stage set, with stairs and a waterfall, a paneled and gilded ceiling, and a fountain shooting real water. Probably these ambitious scraps of decoration hold the metaphor I am searching for to understand the game being played. The hall was a cinema, but now the cinema has been divided into over a hundred cubicles, as if it were a computer-processed television image. Where darkness and silence used to allow for but a single lit surface and but a single source of sound, now there are a hundred surfaces and a hundred sounds. Still, nothing is safe from the future, and soon virtual reality will come sweep aside the video game screens, and only nostalgic rockers or revivalist artists will play in the few arcades that are not converted, like the old jukeboxes, into retropop decoration pieces.

Video game parlors cannot shake off an impression of seediness (a kind of "gambling den effect"). This is true even of the most upmarket, the ones that combine kitsch and the atmosphere of New York's East Side with tin staircases and beaten metal screens, or postmodern advertising signs with the fluorescent colors that were in use a decade ago. Or rather, the parlors put up with this impression as one of the by-products of their scenography. In the suburbs sometimes children are accompanied by their mothers, who look strangely out of place because they do not know what postures they should be adopting, or how to avoid the ricocheting light and sound. They have brought their children to a place that is unavoidable but dangerous, and they think their presence may save their offspring from an addiction that they adjudge frightening precisely because it takes their children away from those real or imaginary places where they can be watched over. The children, controls in hand, are more skillful than their mothers are. They are also more intelligent: The mothers just get lost in the maze of images that is of no interest to them because they fail to understand it, or which they fail to understand for lack of interest. These mothers underline rather than weaken the parlor's seedy impression, because they are there like someone accompanying a drunk to a bar with the impossible aim of making him drink a few glasses less.

Much more than the game machinery, it is this impression of seediness or "gambling den effect" that marks the presence of a subculture whose members valorize achievements the rest of society does not consider to be achievements: for example, defeating the machine, which does not mean defeating a notional equal, but rather defeating something really different; or winning without obtaining anything other than symbolic reward. (When you beat the machines in a casino the rewards are, obviously, material. At some video arcades I have seen bets exchanged, but this is frankly exceptional.) There is, however, also something of the casino in this impression of seediness: Here every player is on his own to decide his own destiny in an individual combat with the machine, to demonstrate to the machine, rather than to the others in the arcade, his skill, fearlessness, cunning, daring, and speed. While it is true that many machines allow for two players to challenge each other, in public arcades the individual player confronting the machine is more common. As in a casino, there may be some observers following the progress of the most skillful or lucky players but, again as in a casino, good manners demand the principle of appropriate conduct: no looking on in a way that might cause the other people to feel as if they were being looked at and, vice versa, no gestures on the part of those who know they are being observed. The intrusive bystander and the braggart stand out badly in the video game landscape.

The impression of seediness also has to do with the general

absence of women. Some do come in following their boy-friends; others who come of their own accord are generally at the screens of games involving geometry, which emit fewer untoward sounds but pose more intellectual difficulties. The latest, three-dimensional, version of Tetris presents real challenges, demanding the ability to anticipate spatial configurations in three planes while you keep a fourth eye on the time to evaluate the speed at which the blocks fall. In any case, women are few and far between and no one looks at them. It is not because they are women that they are ignored, but rather because habit leads you to exchange the fewest possible looks across real spaces: Real spaces dull your sight and make you lose the sharpness and extreme close focus required to see screen space well. Obviously, there are more women at neighborhood arcades (which are more family oriented, smaller, and more restricted in what they offer technically) and at the very large videodromes in the city center—places that stave off the decadence of some once-traditional streets with their lavish decoration and with the presence of security guards, announced in some cases as one of the special services offered by the business's management. But coming across any of these guards immediately reinforces the effect of seediness.

The machines themselves are another thing altogether. Really they are an ensemble of elements belonging to distinct temporalities: The joysticks and control buttons belong to the mechanical age, while the screens belong to the era of digitalized images and sounds. The combination of these two technologies produces a hybrid even more incongruous than a cheap computer's well-designed keyboard. As a result, taking on these machines requires a combination of abilities of distinct types: manipulating the joystick and buttons is firmly part of the order of bodily reflexes; while events on-screen and the desires projected onto the screen pertain to an incorporeal logic. Many games exploit the difficulties produced by this heterogeneity. How much can I accelerate my bodily reflexes in the effort to beat the speed of the silicon chips? What level of difficulty can I take given not only my ability to foresee, abstractly, what will happen next, but more important, my physical capacity to transform this foresight into actions that will appear on the screen? These are the crucial questions for every good video game player. Bad players (which is like saying bad drinkers: those who drink only to get drunk) do not try to answer these questions. Bad players can be detected immediately because they move the joystick like zombies, and press the buttons continuously, without subjecting themselves to the superquick logic of effects and consequences, without changing their tactics. They play out the game to its conclusion as though this conclusion were a question of unavoidable fate, a fate they could never defer temporally, never transform into the goal of a higher score. These bad players (the majority of the players I have seen) are overcome by the speed of the machine and believe that the speed of their physical reflexes will somehow be able to compensate for the fact that everything speeds up on the visual plane. They work against time. A good player, by contrast, works with time: He is only as fast as he need be, never faster than necessary. Bad players go against the logic of the game, which does not lie *only* in physical acceleration but which lies rather in a theory of the encounter (as in ballistics) between the acceleration of movement and the translation of reflexes into decisions that may make the endgame easier. I have very rarely seen good players, but there have now appeared, in the United States, how-to manuals. Players learn little if they submit to a video game as if it were but a television program with a little more interactivity.

There are machines that simulate a bad movie, whose controls imitate pistols or rifles. Though their technology may be more sophisticated, *conceptually* they are the video game's prehistory. The realism of the images these games produce is banal and unbelievable: banal because they translate the original iconic independence of video games' classic images into icons that imitate other icons; unbelievable because the laws of the video game could accept naturalistic realism only if it were perfect (as in virtual reality), not simply an awkward approximation to images that are older than the technology that makes them possible. Few fine players choose these machines whose rules, what is more, are too simple, and whose rough imitativeness offends an imagination, displayed by the better designed games, that is totally freed from any naturalistic referent. On the whole these machines (like those that feature football games in which actually existing teams confront each other) are found near the arcade's entrance, to attract those who are not true enthusiasts and who start to play because the machines remind them of something else, not because the machines give them something totally new.

There are also machines that simulate driving a car on a highway or racetrack. It has to be said that these are childish machines par excellence. Their didacticism means that with only minor programming changes, they could be incorporated into the school curriculum to teach children to drive with due respect for traffic signals, to accelerate appropriately on curves, avoiding any sports cars that try to overtake them all of a sudden. These machines multiply trivial omnipotence and are adaptable to the most predictable of desires. Their didacticism teaches nothing new; the emotion they produce has its origins in a hypertechnological variant of bumper cars. Players who do not understand either the abstraction of a geometrical video game or the stylized iconography invented by Nintendo play these games, which are closer to the imaginary of the market and to television adverts than they are to the videodrome aesthetic.

The classic machines (let us call classics those that, like Pacman, produce their own heroes) are the most original. They make evident the logic of variation and repetition that is the law of the game. They also underscore the fact that a video game's secret lies in a sharp distinction between cycles of activity and an evacuation of narrative meaning. Within each stage you win or lose without altering any overall story; progress consists in accumulating points or in preventing the multiplication of difficulties that arise as possible exits become blocked. There is no story or history; rather there are discrete stages at the end of which the player knows whether he has won or lost.

Classic video games refuse narration: Suspense depends upon the assessments made by player and machine after every change in the screen and every push of the buttons or movement of the joystick. Classic games have stylized characters and objects from the imaginary of cartoons, sports, or action films, but their truth lies more in the characters they invent. It is because of Pacman that there can be airplanes, flying saucers, prehistoric animals, and damsels in distress in other video games. Pacman and Tetris incarnate the ideal type of semiosis to which characters and objects that come from outside the world of the computer chip have had to adapt. Such characters adapt all the better the more they lose any traits belonging to graphic or narrative dimensions that historically preceded the video game. Yet the immediate future already tells us that these classic games will be edged out by the conjunction between films and games. It is when they are out of the picture that, precisely, their quality as classics will be recognized.

It has been said that video games constitute a "carnival of signifiers." This label indicates one attempt to understand the way in which even those games whose title or whose cast of characters promise to provide a story proceed to evacuate narration. In fact, whether or not the promise of narration is kept is unimportant to the player who does not start a game to see if it will reveal the outcome of an almost nonexistent fiction, but who plays rather with the aim that his or her duel with the machine will produce an outcome that is *not fictional*. The presence of signs that conjure up characters, oppositions, hierarchies, enemies, and helpers (as a grotesque structural-folk-televisual model would put it) proves only that you can have a cast of characters without having a story or history. Likewise, each stage of the game contains action without narration. Something about video games pushes them toward the tedium of infinite circularity, just like a Tom and Jerry cartoon's endless play of cat and mouse or Roadrunner's constant flight. There is no need to remember any previous stage in order to pass on to the next. Indeed, a player who stopped to remember would immediately be set back in the race the game insists upon. What takes the place of a story, and the advertising material that comes with these games presents it as a sales pitch, is a *theme,* generally couched from the perspective of the player whom the material converts into the first person: You are an air force pilot who has to complete a mission by flying over unknown mountainous territory, and so on and so forth. There are also "intellectual" games, sold for use on home computers and to court the good conscience of their users who are invited to construct and develop their own plots, and are given time to consider alternatives.

We have, then, theme without narrative—that is, theme in a primitive state before anything has happened, before any detours or subplots. Hence: theme and signifiers. The medium contains a set of repetitions organized into cycles that demand a performance whose truth is not to be found in any confrontation between characters, but rather in the duel between player and machine. In this sense the classic video game produces a nonnarrative plot, composed of an encounter between physical actions and their digital consequences. Many films today imitate, without being able to achieve completely, this emptying out of history. In place of history, they offer the repetition of plot devices. Video games, like these films, split narrative from activity, character from narrative, extracting each from the assemblage that had traditionally brought them together.

If video games are a carnival of signifiers, then this is a carnival of activity without plot, that is specific to an epoch in which the experience of plot tends to disappear. Video games propose the illusion that actions may one day be able to modify the infinite recurrence that is inscribed into the machine and is presented to the potential player on the game's first screen, where his or her alternatives are endlessly repeated. As with televisual *zapping,* here, too, there is something of that combination of speed and erasure that could be the sign of an epoch.

Chapter 2

The Waking Dream

Zapping

The image has lost all intensity. It produces no surprise or intrigue; in the end, it is not especially mysterious or especially transparent. It is there for but a moment, filling up the time it takes to wait for the next image that follows. Likewise this subsequent image fails to surprise or intrigue; it too turns out to lack mystery or even much in the way of transparency. It stays there only a fraction of a second before being replaced by a third image, one that is again unsurprising and unintriguing, as indifferent as the previous two images. This third image lasts an infinitesimal fraction of a second, then dissolves as the screen turns bluish gray. You've intervened by using the remote control. Close your eyes and try to remember the first image: Weren't there people dancing, some white women and black men? Were there also black women and white men? You distinctly remember seeing some long curly hair and a pair of hands tousling and throwing it from the nape of the neck so that it covered a woman's breast, presumably the same woman whose hair it was. Or was that the second image, a closer shot of two or three of the dancers? Was the woman with the curly hair black? She did seem very dark, but perhaps she wasn't black, while the hands playing with the hair were (and so perhaps they were a man's hands). From the third image you remembered other hands, a forearm with bracelets, and the lower part of a woman's face. She was drinking something, from a can. The others carried on dancing behind her. It was hard to tell whether or not the woman drinking was the one with the long, curly hair, but you were sure that it was a woman and that the can was a beer can. Another command from the remote control and the screen lights up again.

One, two, three, four, five, six, seven, eight, nine, fifty-four. There's a close-up of a lion advancing through tropical vegetation; a close-up of an orange oval with black letters against the background of a gas station; a wide shot of a circus ring (though it doesn't seem really to be a circus) full of handwritten placards; a close-up of a woman, three-quarter profile, wearing a lot of makeup, saying "I don't want to listen to you"; two guys leaning on the bonnet of a police car (they're young and they're arguing); a woman's backside, unclothed, moving into the background; a wide shot of a street, in some suburb far from here; Libertad Lamarque about to break into song (though perhaps about to break down in tears rather than into song, because a guy's approaching her and seems to be threatening her); a likable woman making spaghetti for her family while her children and husband are all shouting; one samurai on his knees in front of another, fatter samurai, with Spanish subtitles superimposed on the platform, flush with the screen; another woman heaping up dripping clothes while her mother (you don't know why, but the older woman must be her mother) looks on; Tina Turner in three different poses in three different parts of the screen; then the Mexican singer Alaska, in silhouette (but it's obviously her); a presenter with a squint smiles and shouts; the president of one of those new European republics talking to a reporter in English; two news readers speaking with Spanish accents; Greta Garbo in stockings dancing in a hotel room; Tom Cruise; James Stewart; Alberto Castillo; a close-up of a man turning his head to one side of the screen where you can see part of a woman's face; Fito Páez shaking out his curls; two news readers speaking German; an aerobics class on a beach; a more or less lower-class woman lets out a shout as she looks at the microphone a reporter's pointing toward her; three models sitting in a living room; another couple of models sitting around a coffee table; ten boys surfing; another president; the words *the end* superimposed over a mountainous landscape; a town on fire, with people running carrying bundles of clothes, and some boys strung up by their necks (again, not a scene from around here); Marcello Mastroianni shouts to Sophia Loren, next to a luxury car, on a highway; some children come running into a kitchen and open up the freezer; a symphony orchestra and choir; Orson Welles up on a pulpit, dressed as a priest; Michelle Pfeiffer; an American football game; a game of tennis, women's doubles; two news readers speaking in Spanish but with strange accents; a black person getting punched in the lobby of a bar; two news readers, on the local news, look at each other and laugh; black and white actors in a Brazilian slum speaking Portuguese; Japanese cartoons. A final command from the remote control and the screen returns to bluish gray.

After a while you turn it back on again because it's ten o'clock at night. A very smartly dressed gentleman sitting behind a desk says good evening and gives a quick overview of what will take place over the course of the next two hours of interviews with politicians and personalities of all kinds. After this, a series of shots shows the set: There are artificial plants simulating natural vegetation, and other spiky floral Japanese-style arrangements; spotlights up above; shots of furniture including sofas, sideboards, tables with little coffee cups, flowerpots, and floral arrangements; a contemporary painting; another painting; overhead lights, and again the gentleman promising to return in a few minutes. Remote control. Now commercials: Again the white women and black men dancing; now it is clear that they are in a Caribbean landscape. Remote control: Two actors make stupid faces, put their heads together, and look at each other. Commercials: A car runs along a highway through a mountainous landscape. A forty-something man opens the door to an apartment, startling a seventeen-year-old boy and a girl of the same age. Remote control. The smartly dressed man returns; on his right and left sit a few well-

known politicians along with a woman you don't recognize.
You leave the remote control on the arm of the chair and get
up. From the kitchen you can hear the beginning of the interview. Five minutes later, the smartly dressed man says he'll see
us again after the commercial break. Remote control. News-
flash. Commercials. Situation comedy. Police series. Commercials. A fat man pants while kissing a sleeping woman, who
seems to be having a disturbing dream. Commercials.

A young man (who looks as though he could be Richard
Gere's identical twin) finishes shaving and throws a gleaming
gel-like cologne on his face and bare chest; a remarkably pretty young woman is getting dressed; the man, still shirtless,
wanders around his penthouse, goes to the telephone, stops,
distracted by something or other, picks up a saxophone and
starts to play; the woman is now dressed, in an elegant, formal
style; the man carries on playing the sax in his penthouse; the
woman makes a gesture of annoyance and goes out onto the
street; the man is already on the street with his car and inter-
cepts her; it seems they know each other. A young girl, in a
T-shirt and stockings, walks around the apartment she shares
with her boyfriend or husband; she makes for the bedroom,
looking for something; the bed is unmade and all the while he,
while leaning up against the wall, watches her and smiles; all
of a sudden the girl lifts up the sheets to find a saxophone; she
kneels on the bed and starts to play. The party is at its height,
with everyone exchanging meaningful looks and drinking
something out of glasses with a lot of ice; a honey-colored liq-
uid that looks like caramel flows from bottles; suddenly everyone turns to look toward one corner of the room because a
boy in a white jacket has snatched up his saxophone. In the
film, there's a doctor who works in a mental asylum, where he
has to deal with all the most enigmatic cases, including that of
a madman who, it seems, has come from another planet in
order to show us the truth of our own; at home, as a means of
distraction from all his worries, the doctor also plays the sax.
Tonight's television is like an unanticipated homage to John

Coltrane and Charlie Parker. Any moment now the music video channel will turn to Wayne Shorter.

The combination of a surfeit of images and a relatively simple gadget, the remote control, has enabled the great advance in interactivity seen over the last few decades. This advance has not been the product of any technological development originating from the big electronics corporations; rather it has been brought about by ordinary, everyday consumers. It should be obvious enough that we are talking about *zapping*.

A remote control is a syntactic machine, a handheld editing machine with unpredictable and instantaneous results, the basis for a symbolic power exercised according to laws television has taught its viewers. The first law of television is that in any given period of time, the goal should be to produce as great an accumulation of high-impact images as possible; paradoxically, this law implies either that the amount of information per time period is minimal, or that there is a large amount of undifferentiated information (though it is true that the images provide an "information effect"). The second law demands making the most of all the implications of the fact that, except in cases where a program is first recorded and then submitted to operations that are the province of media experts rather than television viewers, it is impossible to read visual or sound discourses retrospectively, because they unfold in real time. Television exploits this feature of real time discourses, treating it as a quality that allows for images to be repeated with no regard for sense. The medium's speed surpasses our capacity to retain its contents. The medium is faster than what it transmits. One effect of this speed is that audio and video tracks may often clash and finally cancel each other out. The third law of television is that there should be no respite from or holding back of the image flow even for a moment, because such pauses conspire against the form of attention most adequate to the mass media aesthetic, and would affect what is considered its greatest value: its varied repetition of the same. The fourth law is that the ideal edit, though not always possible, should bring together a succession of very brief shots; the camera should be in constant motion in order to fill the screen with an array of different images, and to stave off any change in channel.

Television's success resides in its attention to these laws, but they also make for *the structural possibility of zapping*. Alarmed network executives and advertising agencies see zapping as a threat to viewer loyalty. Yet they would be better off accepting that without zapping nobody these days would watch television. What almost half a century ago was an attraction based upon the image has become an attraction sustained by speed. As it has turned from relying on stationary and unhurried wide shots to the dance of the "switcher," television has constantly developed the possibilities its basic three-camera arrangement allows for cutting and montage, without suspecting that there was a point on this road at which it would have to swallow its own medicine. A remote control is much more than a switcher for amateurs.

The switcher is a weapon in the arsenal of the person directing the camera, who can at the press of a button move from one point of view to another, often without apparent rhyme or reason; the remote control belongs to the arsenal of those watching, who can at the press of a button introduce a cut where the camera directors had not thought to cut, effecting a transition from one incomplete image to another incomplete image produced by another camera, on another channel, or on the other side of the planet. Directors use the switcher to set up an anchor in a set (which may be the news-readers' desk or the presenters' living room, a dance floor or staircase in a musical, the garden or chalet in a soap opera). A remote control does not anchor anyone to any particular place; instead it sets up an irreverent and irresponsible dream syntaxis, product of a postmodern unconscious that mixes together images from all over the planet. Optimists may think that we have reached the apotheosis of the "open work," the limit of aleatory art raiding a giant bank of "ready-made" images. But to reach this conclusion requires the cultivation of a cynical indifference to the problem of these images' semantic density.

Zapping raises a series of interesting questions. There is of course the matter of viewer freedom, and the way it is exercised with the speed of an atomic-powered space transporter running around a shopping mall. Every break in the flow requires a supplementary activity. Images are linked together through contiguity rather than superimposed upon each other, and a reading is based upon syntactic subordination rather than coordination (zapping allows us to read as if every image-sentence were potentially connected by the conjunctions "and," "or," or "nor," or simply separated by ellipsis). Zapping abolishes old laws of visual narration that laid down rules about point of view, about transitions from one type of shot to another that might be closer up or pulled farther back, about the relative duration of takes, about superimposition, sequencing, and fades. What we have now is not Eisenstein's dream of "sovereign montage," but rather the disappearance of montage, in that montage always presupposes that shots conform to a hierarchical organization. Zapping demonstrates that home montage knows but a single authority, and that is the desire that moves the hand pressing the remote control. Like many other phenomena particular to the culture industry, zapping appears to be a full realization of the democratic ideal. It seems to involve editing self-generated by the consumer, cottage industries of productive television viewers, a liberated crew free to run the media space capsule, family cooperatives of symbolic consumption within which authority is ardently discussed, citizens participating in an electronic public sphere, active viewers who use the remote control to contradict old theories about manipulation, zappers taking on the cultural hegemony of the elites, stubborn saboteurs of ratings measurements and, should the occasion present itself, masses ready to rebel against the diktats of mass media capitalists.

Whatever the validity of these claims, it is true that zapping is television's major innovation. But its newness exaggerates something that has always formed part of the medium's logic.

Zapping is simply a more intense version of what commercial television has done from the outset. Zapping was always at the core of televisual discourse, as the mode of production of sequences of images whose point of departure was the presence of more than one camera in the studio. It is a matter of linguistic chance that zapping evokes rapping, musical improvisation on melodic norms or preexisting rhythms, but the idea of televisual zapping does contain something of this improvisation bound by a rigid set of rules. One of these rules would be speed, considered as medium and goal of a so-called visual rhythm that corresponds to short (and ever shorter) concentration spans. Here attention and duration are two complementary and opposed variables, and conventional wisdom has it that it is only by cutting duration that you will manage to generate attention.

Along the way, what has been lost is silence, which was one of the decisive formal elements of modern art (from Miles Davis to John Cage, from Kasimir Malevich to Paul Klee, or from Carl Dreyer to Michelangelo Antonioni). Television, a near contemporary of the avant-gardes, uses their methods but never their constructive principles. There is no need to attack or defend it for this: Television is none the better nor any the worse for having borrowed some or even many of its methods from the century's "high" art. Its aesthetic is its own. Modern art may have produced works in which silence and emptiness demonstrate the infuriating impossibility of speech and show how we need the unsaid for anything to be said, but this is not why the loss of silence, of emptiness, and of blankness affects television.

This loss of silence, and of visual emptiness, is a problem specific to televisual discourse. Yet it is not the nature of the medium itself that imposes this problem, but rather the way in which the medium has been used, the way in which only some of its technical possibilities have been developed while others have been closed off. Rhythmic acceleration, on the one hand, and the absence of silence or of visual emptiness, on the other, are complementary effects. There are risks television is unable to take, because silence or a blank screen (or even concentrating upon a single image) alike go against the culture of perception that television has instituted, a culture echoed and reinforced by its audience through the phenomenon of zapping. Either a single shot that lasts too long or silence on the soundtrack may prompt channel hopping. Market-based television therefore needs what it calls rhythm, although its vertiginous succession of shots constitutes less a rhythmic expression than simply a strategy to avoid zapping. Television puts its trust in the idea that high impact and speed will compensate for the absence of blank spaces and silences, which have to be avoided because they open up the cracks through which zapping slips. We should, however, ask whether in fact things happen exactly the other way around. We should ask whether it is that zapping becomes possible precisely because this overabundant visual discourse has no rhythm; because once all its points are equivalent, the discourse can be cut at any point. It is not television as form, as virtual possibility, that determines that it should be governed by the laws of speed and total temporal satiation; rather it is television as industry, producing commodities at huge cost, that leads it to reduce any risky bets to a minimum.

From all these features of televisual culture arise a specific form of reading and a form of memory. Some image fragments manage to establish themselves in our consciousness with the weight of iconicity, and are recognized, remembered, and cited, while other such fragments are passed by and can be repeated infinitely without boring anybody because, in fact, nobody sees them. These latter images are padding, constituting a gelatinous tide in which other images float and sink, and from which those that have established themselves as recognizable icons then emerge. Icons need this mobile mass of images precisely so they can differentiate themselves from the mass, so they can surprise and circulate at speed. More attractive images require a "contrasting medium." They owe their existence to an army of images that are not remembered, but that pave the way for them. The ever more numerous images that make up this tide of the forgettable are not noticed so long as iconic images exist; when these latter images grow scarce, zapping occurs. All this takes less time to happen than it takes to write about its happening.

The images that make up television's padding are repeated more often than are the "fortunate" images. But these, too, are repeated. Intellectual admirers of the televisual aesthetic recognize that repetition is one of its traits and, with varying degrees of erudition, they trace its origins back to folk culture, to public street spectacles, marionettes, Grand Guignol, nineteenth-century newspaper serials, melodrama, and so on. I am not going to linger on details. It is better that we come to some agreement from the start: Commercial television's serialized repetition *is like* that of other arts and discourses whose prestige has been legitimated by time. Like the newspaper serial, television repeats a structure, a cast of characters, a small ensemble of psychological and moral types, a system of plot devices, and even an arrangement of plot devices.

The enjoyment of repeated, familiar structures is pleasurable and pacifying. This pleasure is perfectly legitimate as much for popular cultures as for the educated elite's customary diversions. Repetition is a machine for the production of quiet happiness, in which the world's semantic, ideological, or felt disorder finds eventual realignment or oases in which order is partially restored. The conclusion of a newspaper's serialized novel sets things back in their place, and this is appreciated even by postmodernity's fractal, decentered subjects. There is no need to reiterate over and over again what has already been said twenty times over about the newspaper serial, all for the sole purpose of seeking out prestigious antecedents for television, when in truth it neither asks for nor needs them. It would be more of an issue to ask whether the aesthetic effects of televisual repetition evoke the seriality of Alexandre Dumas more than they do that of the justifiably forgotten Paul Feval. In other words, nineteenth-century serial novels ranged from those written by Dumas to those written by Paul Feval. When it comes to television, I am very conscious of who could be its

Paul Fevals, but finding its Dumases turns out to be a little trickier. If this comparison brings us to a dead end, we might have to consider that the comparison between television and the nineteenth-century serial novel fails to fit very well. Even Umberto Eco thinks that Balzac is more interesting than the *Dallas* scriptwriters; in fact, only someone who has not seen *Dallas* or has not read Balzac could imagine any possible proof to the contrary.

Given television's novelty, we need to read it using the tools that it itself provides. I started with zapping because that is where televisual discourse's truth lies. Zapping exemplifies a syntactic model (that is to say, the model for a key part of its operation, the way in which one image relates to another) that television set to work long before its viewers invented the "interactive" use of the remote control. Actually existing television in the commercial market has to produce an infinite quantity of broadcast hours per year. So, because its viewers finds themselves obliged to watch too many images, television also has to produce too many. Any *qualitative* relation between two images, from which a third, ideal image would emerge to enable meanings to be built up, is almost an impossibility within the uninterrupted sequence of edits that the market demands of commercial television. It is not, then, that its chance conjunctions of images imply an aesthetic choice that would position television close to aleatory art. Instead, this is a last resort to which television retreats when it has to put hundreds of thousands of images onto the screen each week.

Television's serial repetition is simply a way out of this bottleneck. The hundreds of hours of weekly television (on terrestrial channels and on cable) would be unmanageable were each programming segment to require its own format. This trait of popular literature, of genre cinema, the circus, fairground comedians, folk music, or melodrama (as everybody hastens to remind us, citing still more antecedents whose antiquity is to guarantee prestige) is in fact a response determined by a particular system of production. Seriality guards against any unforeseeable stylistic or structural outlay. In television soaps, the binary system whereby characters are only ever sketched in black and white allows stories to be constructed at the speed demanded by producers who are taping three or four episodes a day. Here, actors know exactly what to expect and scenes repeat a few easily identifiable typologies. Conflicts consist in the confrontation between moral and psychological forces whose predictability is only interrupted by plot complications that, on the one hand, resort to classical topoi and, on the other, actualize these topoi with a set of immediate references that give soaps their themes, taken from the nightly news. The so-called new television of the last few years simply overlays the same decades-old pattern of codified desires with a patchwork of scraps that aim to name reality: political corruption, AIDS, sexual excess, homosexuality, or shady deals in public or private.

A serial aesthetic needs a simple system of traits whose condition is that nuances should be eliminated. Psychological and moral Manichaeism lowers the level of problematization and sutures the cracks opened up by formal and ideological sloppiness. The intellectual fashion that, some years ago now, began as an interest in radio and television soap kitsch and then ended up simply consuming it, fails to reply in any convincing way to indictments of mass culture, even to those judgments that demonized it often without knowing anything about it. It should not be enough to oppose to the elitism of those positions most critical of mass culture, simply their symmetrical inversion under the figure of a neopopulism seduced by the charms of industrial culture.

Variety programs, comedies, children's programs, and music programs make serial repetition into a durable canvas (a kind of phantasmal script outline as rigid as if it were made of iron) that improvisation then adorns with its repetition in variation. This tempered novelty is functional for the whole productive system, from scriptwriters to actors. Moreover, it makes economic sense, because by allowing sets and costumes to be used over and over again, it guarantees that any time investment need only be minimal. Television is loathe to give up on anything that has passed the test of efficiency, and this in no way goes against its interrupted image flow but rather, precisely, is what makes it possible. Very good and very bad programs can be made in serial units: The use of seriality does not in itself guarantee results. It does, though, ensure a mode of production in which repetition makes up for any points at which improvisation (on the part of actors or technicians) breaks down. Yet, and however unpleasant it may seem to bring this up, repetition not only supports but also banalizes the actors' improvisations and becomes no more than a strategy to get out of a jam in dutiful accord with televisual production's greed for time. As in any other art form, improvisation is not so much a substantial quality as it is an ensemble of technical and rhetorical operations. The question of whether it is television comedians or soap opera actors who work most faithfully at improvisation reveals much less about the influence of a theatrical innovation now several decades old than it says about the mode of production in market conditions. Televisual improvisation follows the logic of capitalist serial production more than it corresponds to any aesthetic logic.

Televisual styles very obviously bear the marks of serialized discourse. Comedies, dramas, regionalist programs, and entertainment programs all conform less to a typology of genres (for which psychosocial conflict would be contrasted with an emphasis on the vicissitudes of sentiment, crime mysteries, or the foregrounding of youth, dancing, or music) than they do to a *standard style*: the show. This standard style owes its origins to variety shows, such as comic, music hall, or circus shows. Now the show is the mode of organization for all other stylistic formations: There are news shows, documentary shows, sports highlights shows, political shows at night differentiated from the midday show and the midafternoon show, drama shows, children's shows, comedy shows, and talk shows dealing with the intimacy of people's innermost feelings. The common denominator is miscellaneousness.

This standard style founds *televisuality*. Those who appear on television have to adapt to it, and so politicians, for example, seek to construct their public personae according to its logic and, therefore, to memorize lines of dialogue, gestures, and verbal rhythms. They have to be expert at rapid transitions, changes in speed and direction to stave off audience boredom. The televisual politician's skills are honed in the medium itself, which functions like a school handing out certificates of electronic charisma. It is not just actors, but also anyone who appears on the screen who has to master the condition of televisuality. This mastery has the same importance that being photogenic had in Hollywood's classic period. Televisuality ensures that images belong to the same system of visual representation, by homogenizing them and making them instantly recognizable. It allows for variety because it undergirds the profound unity that sutures the discontinuities between different programs (and advertising collaborates fully in this task). Televisuality is the fluid that gives television its consistency and that ensures immediate recognition on the part of its audience. As long as due respect is shown, certain rules can be bent: Some electronic intellectuals retain a certain tone, imported from academia or print journalism, that maintains televisuality's allure without bowing to its commoner forms. This tone makes its difference felt. Standing up to the daily hubbub, it opens up a calm parenthesis challenging the "tyranny of time" and demonstrating that television does not necessarily preclude an hour of reflection from time to time, so long as certain characteristics are maintained. These indispensable features include strong iconic presence, the arbitrary camera movements to which we are all habituated, digitalized images, an attentive ear to what the viewing public has to say, and an appeal to sentiment.

Television shares in what it has already shared out, and what it shares out is in fact what it has picked up in all sorts of places, but always according to the principle that just as the viewing public is television's best interpreter (hence the power of ratings for market-based television), so too television has to know its audience at least as well as its audience knows television. Functioning as a democratic and plebeian mirror, mirroring the totality of viewing publics and starting also to reflect each of its fragments, television constitutes its referents as the viewing public, and its viewers (the public) as referent. How then can we begin to answer the question of whether the public speaks like the star system's celebrities or whether celebrities speak like their viewers?

These traits of televisuality can protect televisual discourses from the discontinuity brought about by zapping. At any point you always know where you are, and can abandon one program to move on to another with the guarantee that what is happening elsewhere will also be intelligible. We vote with the remote. Competition between channels consists of a struggle to occupy the (imaginary) space where zapping might be brought to a halt. All in all, images signify less and less and, paradoxically, are more and more important. From the point of view of form, though television may seem happily victorious over the entire discursive field, in fact it has come to a crossroads.

Live Recording

The following is a dialogue seen and heard, one late afternoon, on a current affairs program put out by a state channel.

PRESENTER: This program throws up surprises all the time. Coming up is one of the strangest so far. We will present it with all due care. This gentleman came to the station saying that he had just killed someone, and that he wanted to give himself up on camera . . .

UNNAMED MAN: I don't know if I killed him. We fought and I defended myself.

PRESENTER: Tell me all about it.

MAN: Yesterday afternoon my wife and I were drinking a fair amount of wine with friends when some of them started to make fun of my wife because she's got a harelip. And this kid started to take the Mickey out of the way my wife speaks. I told him he'd better not provoke me. Look, I'm a good person, I think of myself as a good person. At this point a couple of neighbors come and tell him that what he's doing doesn't go down well with my personality. My personality, I recognize that I've got a fairly strong personality. And I tell him let's fight it out. I give him a couple of slaps and then we're fighting. There were something like three of them, and I was on my own. I don't remember exactly.

PRESENTER: What happened next?

MAN: They hit me, they kicked me in the head. They broke open my mouth. Look how my lip's cut up.

PRESENTER: Why are you giving yourself up? Why have you come here?

MAN: Well . . . I had nowhere to go, and I don't think of myself as a murderer or at least . . .

PRESENTER: But did you or didn't you kill someone?

MAN: Well . . . I hurt him. I don't know if the boy's alive. I hope he's alive.

PRESENTER: Do you think you killed him?

MAN: I don't know, I don't . . .

PRESENTER: What did you hit him with?

MAN: With a knife.

PRESENTER: You know that now you'll be taken away and arrested.

MAN: It doesn't matter; I believe in justice.

What makes this dialogue different from the one this man would have had if he had gone to a police station? The question is simple enough. But if we can find an answer, we go straight to the point of how television can seem to be a space that is closer to us than is the neighborhood police station, and how a program presenter becomes a more trustworthy figure than a duty officer would be. I want to go beyond the most obvious explanation, that the poor are all too well acquainted with the police's violent side. There is more to this question than this explanation suggests. The program excerpt I cited brings together all the characteristics of the new television, or what has also been called relational television. There is, first of all, the fact that it is a live recording; then, that it is a slice of life presented with a clarity of which a nineteenth-century naturalist writer or a nonfiction writer in our own century could only have dreamed; third, the fact that a television studio appears to the protagonist to be safer, more accessible, and more appropriate than any state institution. Finally, there is the fact of the ever present equalizing extension of television's frame of reference, producing in its viewers the belief that we are all, potentially, objects and subjects who could appear on camera.

Let us break this down. Live recording is the extreme limit no filmic documentary can reach, precisely because the technology of the cinema makes it impossible. With film, even the most direct recordings always have a deferred reception. The lag between capturing an image and its projection may be cut to its minimum, but still time passes between the two events. And time here is not neutral. In the course of its passing, technical operations take place (development, editing, and duplication), by means of which the image undergoes a process made up of manipulations that are indispensable for the filmic image's visibility. The fact that these necessary manipulations exist then opens up a field of doubts about what we could call "unnecessary" manipulations, which might be attributable to chance or to design. We find ourselves asking how much of the negative was not printed and, as a result, how many images seen by the director are we ourselves not seeing? What cuts were made during editing, and for what motives? If a cut seems inevitable for technical reasons, as, for example, with an image that is too blurred or out of focus, we may wonder who made these judgments about quality and how. But we can also suppose that other cuts were made for reasons never completely specified: A director may think that a scene lasts too long, that a panoramic establishing shot is unnecessary, or that a long shot should be cut in order to highlight the graphic nature of the subject by means of whatever close-up is finally chosen. A photographer unhappy with the light in a particular image can intervene in the course of its development or duplication, and we will never know whether or not this has happened, just as we will never be able to tell whether or not what we are seeing in the film is exactly what was printed on the negative. Anything can happen in the lag between a film's recording and its projection, and this "anything" opens up the possibility that fiction, or the tendentious opinions of those who made the film, will sneak in, or that mistakes will be covered up in the editing room. The temporal distance built into film production gives birth to suspicion.

Television is subject to this suspicion so long as its transmission is not *live*. With a recorded tape it is likewise possible to carry out operations such as editing, light correction, superimpositions, fades, or to put together a battery of images with no respect for the order in which they were captured by the camera. But, unlike cinema, television has access to a singular possibility: *live recording combined with live broadcast.* Here, image manipulations, though they still take place, do not have time on their side: What you see is literally "real" time, and so whatever the camera sees, the viewer sees, too. Now, it is not quite as simple as this, because there is room for technical and stylistic intervention (involving lighting, depth of field, decisions about framing and what is to be left offscreen, transitions from one camera to another, recording interruptions during commercial breaks), yet everything takes place *as if* it were. The audience chooses to disregard the possibility of intervention, and the televisual institution reinforces its credibility by effacing any distortion of events when it resorts to live recording that is broadcast live.

Hence the birth of an illusion: That what I see is what is, at the moment I see it. I see what *is* now, not what once *was*, broadcast later. I see existence's progress and time's passage. I see things as they are, not things as they were. I see without anyone's showing me how I should see what I see, because images recorded live and broadcast live give the impression that they have not been edited. Real time annuls spatial distance. If what I see is time passing, the spatial distance that separates me from that time can be bracketed off. I see, therefore, *as if* I were there. At its outset, television was limited to this live recording sent out live, which was not a choice but a constraint. From commercials to soap operas, everything went out live. Later, the perfection of the technology enabling broadcast to be deferred beyond the moment of recording allowed for rehearsal, for what had come out badly to be repeated, for editorial intervention, and for experimentation with formats. Live recording sent out live stopped being a necessity, to become a choice displaying what television *can do* and not simply what it had once been obliged to do for technical reasons alone.

So now it is possible to choose between one type of recording and another, and between deferred or live broadcast. The obligatory live recording of television's earliest days has been transformed into a new possibility. At this point, it acquires other values and functions. Live discourse's illusion of truth is (to date) the most powerful strategy known through which to produce, reproduce, present, and represent "the real." It gives the impression that there is nothing between the image and its material referent, or at least that there are very few interventions, and what interventions there are seem neutral because they are considered technical. Faced with live recording, it is possible to think that the camera eye alone is in charge—and how would one distrust something as socially neutral as a lens? At this point, live recording seems to do away with the centuries-old debate over the relation between world and representation.

The consequences of this are manifold. Because the fact is that a lens is a world away from neutrality. And that even when a recording is absolutely live, staging is still an issue. The camera still decides what will be in the frame and therefore what will stay offscreen, while the way the camera moves in or out injects drama into or defuses conflict from images, and offscreen sound provides information that combines with what the image shows. All this happens even if those making the recording are not particularly conscious of their choices. And if program makers do not consciously consider their options, by default such decisions are left to ideology and to the aesthetics of the medium that speaks loud and clear when everything else is mute.

The truth effect of live recording only adds to the greater powers of conviction accorded to images over words on their own. There is nothing intrinsically wrong with images; it is just that they have that capacity of seeming more immediate than any other discourse. In a culture built on vision, images have more persuasive force because they are not limited, as discourse can be, to being simply credible or coherent. They convince because they just seem real: Things seem real when you see them with your own eyes, more than when you have to rely on somebody else's telling you. Live recording places the viewer within the camera eye, and nobody has to tell you anything because it is *as if* you had been there. It may even be better still than being there, because you would not have been able to come in so close to pick up an imperceptible expression with the clarity of a close-up, or perhaps you would have been distracted by less important details that the camera has removed from the frame.

This is why a man would confess to murder in front of a television camera: As a viewer of television, he wants to occupy a space of truth in which his words will sound more believable. He says that he trusts in justice, but he has not gone to a judge to confess. He thinks that among all institutions, live television is most worthy of his trust. Here no one will be able to twist either his gestures or his statement and, what is more, no police officer will be able to force him to say more than he wants to say, or to leave him isolated for hours. Television has become guardian of his habeas corpus.

Viewers, for their part, are given what they have been seeking: not more verisimilitude (which is a product of discursive and rhetorical operations), but life, live and direct. They are given "happenings," that is, events as they become events. Such events become more valuable the more distrust is aroused by other public events whose laws and actors, and whose institutions' working guidelines, are not well known (in other words, all those practices that, like politics, cannot always be shown *while* they take place). Through happenings, on the other hand, television constructs a mode of presentation extending and improving the level of realism (all things considered, fairly high) possessed by other formats. Happenings broadcast live are differentiated from live recordings played back later, as habitually used by news shows, in that a news show's live recordings have been foreseen (and seen in advance) by someone, somewhere in the television station. So the syntactical connections for these deferred live recordings do not simply arise spontaneously. With happenings recorded live and sent out live, however, the illusion is produced that there is no narrator. Characters make themselves heard without any filter or mediation other than that of the televisual institution itself that, here, seeks to erase its traces.

This live-live happening is a fragment of life legitimating not only the images it itself contains, but also, by proxy, all televisual images. Its truth effect is powerful enough to spill over to other live recordings whose broadcasts are deferred and even to broadcasts that are not recorded live. The truth of television lies in live recording broadcast as it happens, not only because this is its original technical novelty, but also because it grounds an argument for the medium's trustworthiness. In the face of the ever increasing opacity of other public institutions, and in the face of the infernal complexity of public problems, television presents *what happens, as it happens* and, framed like this, things always seem truer and simpler. Invested with an authority that the church, political parties, and the school system have now lost, television resounds with the voice of a truth that everyone can pick up on without much effort. Televisual epistemology is, in this sense, as much realist as it is populist, and it has unleashed a devastating practical critique of all the paradigms of knowledge transmission with which educated, literate culture is familiar.

Television's pact with the viewing public rests upon this *ideological appeal to common sense*, and no one would dare to exhume elitist arguments to criticize it. Television is part of a profane world in which there no longer exist authorities whose power is based only on tradition, revelation, or myths of origin. While it may institute other myths and other authorities, it does so not through a restitution of the past but by configuring the present and, like it or not, probably the future. Television tends toward egalitarianism because, to date, the form in which it has competed in the market is based on audience ratings. Ratings define the policies of the terrestrial channels—despite the fact that some smart advertising people are of the opinion that above a rating of ten points, all that can be sold is the electricity needed to keep the television sets on, rather than the commodities advertised. The same ratings-driven policies also hold sway with cable and pay-per-view television, though here evaluating the audience is more concerned with how it breaks down into segments.

The "new television" is concentrated in formats such as the talk show, and participatory programs, in other words formats that *by definition* are impossible without the public in the studio and in front of the cameras. They differ from a more archaic type of program that might have been based on contests between members of the viewing public or might have allowed the public into the studio, but that did not carry these practices over to the rest of the programming. Nowadays, by contrast, even the most reflective political discussion programs have a studio audience, invite the public to phone in, and put nonexperts around the table precisely for their attributes of nonexpertise. In the spirit of Andy Warhol's oft-repeated *boutade,* television promises us that we will all be on camera sometime because there are no specific qualities but rather "circumstances" that can put us on television. Should circumstances be lacking, that fact that we are citizens is condition enough to be there. In this respect, commercial television feeds off a powerfully leveling and egalitarian imaginary. But it is not this imaginary alone that keeps it going.

The reason we can all be in front of the camera lies in the fact that there are key figures to act as "anchors." If television were only to show us ourselves, it would turn into a hyper-realist nightmare. But quite to the contrary, it also shows us its stars—beings who are exceptional, but who at the same time also speak a language that is completely familiar, and are not averse to everyday banalities. We have here a "mirror culture" that reflects its viewing public through the mediation of the star system's aura. This paradoxical twist to television's demo-cratic urges founds a common culture that enables television to be seen as a space that is both mythic (home of the stars, the true stars of mass society) and, *at the same time,* homely. Venus is in our kitchen; we are allowed into Venus's kitchen. The viewing public can talk informally to the stars, addressing them by their first names. We put our trust in them because of their electronic homeliness, and because stars look to base their charisma not on distance and difference, but in ideologi-cal and sentimental intimacy.

Television presents stars and their public as though we were all cruising through the same cultural continuum. This community of meanings reinforces an imaginary that is simul-taneously egalitarian and paternalistic. The public resorts to television aiming to secure what state institutions cannot guar-antee to provide: justice, compensation, and attention. It is hard to say whether or not television is more effective than other institutions in settling these demands. But there is no doubt that it seems more effective, in that it has no need to ad-here to the prolongations, statutory waiting periods, and for-mal proceedings that otherwise defer or adjourn obligations. The world of television is like a game of squash: The ball may not necessarily bounce back to where you want it to go, but at least it does always bounce back to you. The world of state in-stitutions, even at its very best, does not and never could have this instantaneous quality. The world of television thrives on impulsiveness, while the world of state institutions fulfills its functions adequately when it takes collective impulses and processes them efficiently. The world of television is fast and appears to be transparent; the world of state institutions is slow and its procedures (which are precisely the procedures that make institutional existence possible) are complicated to the point of opacity, thus making people lose hope in them.

Though it might be possible to show that it is in fact no better than state institutions when it comes to providing more reliable or better public service, television feeds off what its viewing public attributes to it and, perhaps, in the short term may give this public some part of what they are looking for. The alleged killer we saw earlier, running to the television station to turn himself in, feels that it can offer more guarantees than can the institutions of law and order. His perception is that it can guarantee to be faster than the bureaucratic machine, that the publicity his actions attract will guarantee greater personal security, that there is a chance of help for his family who will be left alone while he is in prison, and that television can function as a lawyer working on his behalf for free and showing more interest in his case than would a public defender assigned by the State. This is televisual paternalism, flourishing at a time when political paternalism in the big cities can no longer guarantee everyone the contracted services that it used to apportion to all when the social arena was not so overpopulated. Replacing the political caudillo, who used to act as intermediary between the faithful masses and state institutions, the televisual star is a *mediator without a memory,* who forgets everything between one commercial break and another. A star's power does not reside in providing solutions to a protected constituency's problems, but in offering a space in which claims can be asserted and, also, symbolic reparations awarded. Like the lonely men and women who go on television programs looking for a partner, the forgotten and the rejected look to television in search of the hearing that they have found nowhere else.

Television acknowledges its viewing public because, among other reasons, it needs to provide this acknowledgment in order to make its viewers, effectively, its public. The medium's capitalist dynamic ignores everything that could differentiate television from the viewing public and, as a result, hinders the development of any strategies that would only pay off in the long term (which are the type of strategies to which the publishing and music industries have to turn, given that they operate in an always unstable equilibrium balanced between the market's tastes and the risks of investments without immediate returns). Reciprocally, the public finds that television offers them an opportunity to make their voices heard, an opportunity that state institutions do not seem to grant to people at the margins of society, to those who find themselves in exceptional situations, to those who lack the knowledge needed to make their way through the meanderings of government, to those who distrust political mediation, or to those who have failed in their attempts to be heard elsewhere. The name of the game for television is transparency, and as part of this game it responds to demands with speed and efficiency, personalized intervention, and an attention to the expressions of subjectivity and particularism that its public does not find anywhere else. Television's subjects love intimacy (even if this intimacy is imaginary), and television keeps telling them that it alone is close to them. To those stuck in the maelstrom of interpersonal relations found in big cities, television promises imaginary communities in which those skeptical about the possibility of founding or strengthening other communities now live.

There are even those who think that the act of sharing a television set, installed in living room or kitchen as if it were some technological totem, creates new ties, bringing together those who sit in front of the same screen. A new age of video families would mean the reconciliation once more of families that have been pitched to the edge of dissolution by declining authority and deteriorations in paternal and filial relations, but would now be brought back together by the light of television's warm color glow. It is difficult to decide whether or not this beautiful neoanthropological fiction has any truth to it, beyond its good intentions.

There is, however, no reason to doubt the fact that these days the older generation may be familiar with and listen to certain youth subculture heroes. It is television that has brought about this intergenerational familiarity, and when it puts the youth's heroes in this position, it ensures they do not have the subversive or simply antiadult potential their counter-cultural predecessors had when they were confined to films and records. Just as television tends to create points of con-nection between social classes, so it also crosses some bound-aries of age and gender: Programs for adolescents are watched by children and by the old; soap operas may move, with only slight changes, to the evening schedules; and plugs for the day's or the week's programming are shown at more or less any time, putting specific images into circulation among non-specific audiences. Zapping's aleatory syntax leads to encoun-ters, however fleeting, between pensioners and music videos, between cooking shows and men looking for the worldwide sports roundup, or between heavy-metal fans and television evangelists.

At certain times of day, there are millions of us in the same city or country all watching television. This shared vision pro-duces something that goes beyond ratings figures. There can be no doubt that this shared viewing produces a rhetorical sys-tem whose tropes pass into everyday discourse. If television speaks like us, we also speak like the television. In the most evanescent moments of the everyday culture of consumption, television's jokes, forms of speech, and personalities form part of a set of tools whose mastery assures belonging; if you are unfamiliar with them, you must be either a snob or an out-sider. Even members of the intellectual elite, when not engaged in condemning or seeking refuge from television, find it amus-ing to cultivate clichés learned from watching TV (turning to it to find out finally what it is all about, now that everyone else is watching it, or because their taste for kitsch never completely died out in the sixties). Television clichés act as passwords into everyday language, from where, often enough, television took them in the first place only to return them to now-universal use. These days, fashion and changes to the latest "look" of the moment are derived from television more than from film. Exercise classes teach women how to model their bodies to be like those that appear on television, and television has also helped legitimate the cosmetic use of plastic surgery by holding out an ideal mirror in which age differences are more and more indeterminate. Television is not the sole operative pole of attraction for any of these advances in identificatory processes, but television does listen out for what the public has seen on the screen and then record it again and generalize it, pushing it forward only to listen out for it again, and so on continually in a circle, combining production and hermeneutics, in which it is difficult to locate any true point of origin.

Society is now televisual; we live in a "state of television." But contrary to the neopopulist ideology that sees in the small screen an energy whose influence could restore the social ties modernity has corroded, we should ascertain the extent to which television requires a society where these social ties are weak, so it can present itself to that society as the true defender of a democratic, electronic community threatened and scorned by those who do not hear its voice or care about its petitions. I am not saying that this ideology is necessary for the existence of any sort of television "whatever"; I am saying, rather, that it suits television as we know it today. The mimetic relation between television and its viewing public is not, and probably no complete fusion would be, the best that can happen to the world within postmodernity. In this superimposition, any possible critique of actually existing television is forever closed off by accusations of outmoded elitism or professorial vanguardism.

Tied to the mirroring mechanism of the ratings system, television can only put forward a culture of mirroring, in which everyone is to be able to recognize themselves. This "everyone" is precisely television's ideal subject. Terrestrial channels' target is to appeal to the greatest number of people possible, while the objective of cable channels is to broaden their audience share to include all who might potentially be interested in the niche they inhabit. At the moment, though this may not necessarily be a permanent characteristic, television's desire is for fragmented spaces to become either universalized or saturated. To achieve this desire, the new "relational" or "participatory" model installs itself in the cracks left by the dissolution of other social ties and of other participatory movements. The point at which democracy complicates institutional mechanisms and dissolves face-to-face relations provides television with a field in which it can be a medium that both operates at a distance and that also, paradoxically, finds one of its virtues in the representation of intimacy.

From any point of view, television is *accessible*. It reflects and is reflected in its viewing public, setting up something like a structural *mise en abîme* that would confirm all the baroque traits many claim to find in the postmodern condition. Television is secular and its sentiments democratic, but it also has elements that are strongly attached to myth. It compensates for the fact that this world lacks gods by building an Olympus of disposable little icons that are ephemeral but have the power of demigods, so long at least as they hold on to the auratic quality they owe to television. In the face of the aridity of a disenchanted world, television brings a dose of fantasy custom-made for daily life.

It also has other effects that are hard to differentiate from the foregoing. It contributes to the erosion of traditional modes of legitimation, because it gives voice to everything its viewing public desires, and its viewing public's desire is now beyond the control of the principles that once governed or seem to govern it. Mimetic and hyperrealist, television constructs its viewing public to be able then to reflect it, and reflects it to be able then to construct it. At this circle's boundary, television and the public agree on a minimum aesthetic and ideological program. For the purposes of producing this program in televisual terms, all that has to be done is to read the script provided by the viewing public; for its production as a public program, all that has to be done is to read the script that television provides. The viewing public then uses television however seems best or however it can; and television does not shirk from doing the same. The media market, which portrays us all as fictitiously equal, rests upon this pact whose necessity does not derive from the medium's technical possibilities but rather from the capitalist law of supply and demand. The relation of forces is so unequal (and so satisfactory) that nothing will change without some outside intervention. But who would want to do this in these times of market liberalism and depopulated populism?

Politics

Anything it can convert into a theme, from sexual mores to politics, television makes part of its self-reflexive circle. Moreover, any themes it does not touch, from sexual mores to politics, it reduces to dusty neglect. The first image transmitted by Argentine television (which is essentially what I have been talking about in the course of this discussion) was a photograph of Eva Perón. This transmission took place on October 17, 1951, during an experimental transmission that shortly preceded regular broadcasting. The choice of this first television icon (despite being the image of someone who did not live to see the television era) is unsurprising. Evita incarnated politics in its sexualized form, and her photogenic qualities were suitably televisual. With Evita's image, Argentine television proclaimed its first manifesto: Everything shown on the small screen should be touched by an aura. Evita's image brought together the aura of charisma with that of youth and beauty. From that point onward the road to contemporary televisual politics would be long and full of detours, but its origin incorporated a gesture that was, unintentionally, doubly foundational.

Politics today exists only insofar as it is also television. There can be no place for nostalgia for past (and probably hypothetical) direct forms of politics. All that can be done is to mount the most radical possible critique of actually existing video-politics.

The desire for a society in which the truth of social relations could be discerned immediately by all its participants, in which all communication would be ever simple and direct, and in which the artificial contrivances that constitute politics should appear unnecessary, is in the end an anticultural desire. Years ago television invented a female character, let us call her Doña Rosa, who embodied this desire to the point of hyperrealist caricature. Doña Rosa did not care how her objectives were achieved. She did not care what others might be suffering as a result of the attention paid to her demands, nor did she care what values might ever be at stake except insofar as they coincided with the reduced moral code that was hers. Doña Rosa therefore rejected politics, which, precisely, can be defined in opposition to this Darwinian primitivism suitable only for those in a position to defend their rights (or what they consider their rights) through superior force and persistence.

For someone like Doña Rosa, deliberative and institutionalized politics are an obstacle rather than a means to an end. She therefore attacks politicians, distrusting not only their intentions but also, more radically, their very existence. She sees politicians as separating citizens from the realization of what they need. Politics, moreover, is artificial from the perspective of social subjects' desires, assumed to be *natural*. Doña Rosa partakes of a common sense that could only be called liberal in some exaggerated parody: She thinks that any system is illegitimate if it does not make its highest priority the realization of individual rights that she thinks are beyond discussion. Doña Rosa's relation with the State and its institutions is uncompromising. First of all, she thinks that the fact that she pays taxes gives her the power of line-item veto on the national budget. She has seen too many U.S. television programs in which citizens affirm their right not to belong to the national community except in its guise as source of tax revenue. This *fiscal conception of citizenship,* taken to its extreme, conflicts with any notion of equality: Those who pay more have more rights to cash in, and those who pay less ought to accept the poverty of their position. Doña Rosa understands little of this, and in any case it does not interest her. In fact, her idea of citizenship is tied more to economics than it is to civics or to politics; its definition turns on use rather than on exercise, and it is based on rights alone rather than on a combination of rights and responsibilities.

Doña Rosa is only imaginable in a world of mass media politics (though her forebears can be found among the petty bourgeoisie of nineteenth-century realist novels). The politics that interests her is a construction of communicators, her agenda is set by the television news, and she withdraws her trust from her representatives only to let it be administered by the mass media's moguls. In place of the culture of parliamentary discussion, which Doña Rosa cannot stand because she accuses Parliament of unbearable slothfulness, arises the culture of television roundtables in which journalists lecture politicians (on liberal, progressive, democratic, or reactionary themes), and intelligent politicians try to seem less intelligent and more honest than they actually are, because they know that, along with Doña Rosa, the viewing public has learned that there is almost only one universal truth: Politicians are always corrupt.

Though it may today be impossible to imagine politics without television, we can still imagine changes within video-politics. There is no inescapable fate written into television's script. It is not some inevitable item of faith that politicians themselves are of little interest, and that they should therefore make the transition to some style demanded of them by television if they want, first, to appear on the screen and, second, to establish mutual dialogue with their fellow citizens. Having said this, it would be good if we could first convince politicians themselves on this score, so that they might then convince their image consultants who, like diligent master-slaves, tell politicians how, when, and what to say on radio and television.

Politicians' identities are not constructed in the media alone. By submitting completely to the call of the media jungle, politicians give up on what made them politicians: their being the expression of a will broader than their own and *at the same time* their working to mold that will. It is precisely because politics is less about immediacy than it is, much more, about construction and imagination, that it can be said that politics is what should make problems visible, to root out the conflicts involved in their occlusion, for the sake of exposing them to the light of a public arena where they may be defined and find resolution. Now, if conflicts are not allowed to emerge through political means, the media take the place of politics and suggest other, prepolitical or antipolitical, steps toward their resolution. Politics has its diagnostic stage and its decisive productive moment. At both stages the relation between politicians and citizens today needs the media as setting, but there is no inevitable need for mass media presenters to act as mentors. If issues of importance for large majorities of people are turned into nothing but media events, politics and politicians will appear to have no clear meaning for any of us.

Citation

At the same time every week, two actors perform a sketch on a comedy program. The lead actor is fast, canny, and flashy yet discreet at the same time. The second actor is at his side, feeding him opportunities for witty replies, pretending to be smarter than the lead but always showing how much less he himself understands, although in fact he is the one responsible for the sketch's development. The source of the comedy lies in the relationship between these very different men (who in real life are the closest of friends). The sidekick skillfully but unostentatiously lays the foundation for the final piece of repartee that will make the other one look good; his mission, repeated week after week, is to lay the groundwork for the joke's punchline so that the sketch ends in a comic explosion. Sometimes a young, barely dressed woman intervenes only to become the butt of a banal, but just as effective, repertory of jokes, innuendos, double entendres, looks, gropes, and, depending on the night, offensiveness stirred up by the conventional mixture of sexual display and candor. As always, improvisation contributes to the comic effect, and the actors often look at the camera, allude to what is going on offscreen, and pretend to (or really) forget their lines, letting out comments under their breath to tell us that something unforeseen (some more personal subtext between the two actors) has crept into the sketch's script.

Tonight, after the woman, a third actor, much less famous than the first two, enters the scene. In the general atmosphere of apparently directionless improvisation created by the protagonist and his sidekick, the third actor thinks he is allowed to abandon the lines written for him in the script, and he makes up a response of his own to one of the protagonist's lines, stealing the show from the actor who usually sets up the punchline. The latter cuts him down without hesitation: "That's my job as sidekick, not yours as bit-part player."

This retort, completely unscripted, discloses the existence of a strong dialogical structure that, in turn, is determined by a hierarchy among the actors. The retort puts everything back in its accustomed place. In a sketch full of misunderstandings, the sidekick did not let the doubly improvised misunderstanding usurping his place pass him by. The program's technical crew loudly applaud the resolution of this microconflict. The whole episode is undergirded by the *metafictional character* that the program presents as one of its most original virtues. The sidekick's improvised retort lays bare the sketch's ground rules that should, at least in theory, remain hidden. Yet flaunting these ground rules, as this program customarily does, accentuates the comic illusion, rather than destroying it. We laugh at the joke that comes from the script, and we laugh (even more) at the scathing way in which a minor actor has been put in his place by a more senior actor who is cunning, fast, and, what is more, a friend of the protagonist. The protected hierarchy of the performers' commercial value has been laid out in the open, and rather than producing an estrangement that could frustrate the comic effect, it underlines it. There are now two jokes to laugh at. This improvised joke (which is metafictional and self-reflexive because it refers to a hierarchy among the actors that preexists the sketch) appeals to our complicity, and as such it acknowledges that we also need certain skills to process the weekly repartee. Understanding the improvised joke requires much more knowledge than is needed simply to laugh at the joke in the script. Whoever laughs at "That's my job, not yours" is fully aware of how the program works. In our understanding the retort, we, the viewers, become more like the two actors (in this case a pair of true television idols) however much this in some sense distracts us from the comic fiction. We laugh *with* television and not *at* it. We are all included in the tribe to some extent, and there is a redistribution of that authority that accrues to those who know the way things work—neither scriptwriter, director, nor protagonist can stop the sidekick from retorting and so revealing the program's ground rules. Still more energizing is the fact that viewers like us realize what is going on. This awareness is a consequence of the fact that by watching this program and others like it, we have not only learned to laugh, but we have also learned these programs' laws of production. Our laughter is doubled: We laugh because we get the joke, and also because we know why we laugh.

The air of familiarity with which television addresses its viewing public and the imaginary intimacy that the viewing public establishes with television both mine a resource that offers a guarantee of transparency: *self-reflexivity.* Television is always taking us behind the scenes, and not simply when it invites the viewing public into the studios or when it puts some of us in front of the camera. These are like guided visits that function to bring us closer but not to *interiorize* us. Self-reflexivity, by contrast, is the means by which television interiorizes its audience by showing them *how television is made.* What started as an improvised expedient on the part of a few actors and presenters at a time when most, by contrast, made every effort to hide the traces of what was being done and insisted on presenting television as something "ready-made," is now a classic stylistic trait whose productivity is beyond dispute. Television's own self-presentation hinges upon the fact that it is recorded live (even when it is broadcast at a later date) and therefore cannot erase the signs of this live quality; nor does it want to. These signs have become so much its characteristic that they persist in prerecorded programs. All comedy programs are self-reflexive, while news programs are full of self-reflexive commentary about the efforts undertaken to obtain their news images. Even serious current affairs programs make a feature of their own ratings figures; thus their view of themselves is what they see reflected in the mirror of audience choices. Presenters never hesitate to mention technical problems, organizational blunders, or what is taking place behind the camera. Chat-show guests and hosts refer to what was happening just before the show started, revealing the conditions of production of what we are about to see. A channel's owner may break in during the middle of a take and show the truth of his power onscreen. We regularly see cameras moving around, getting ready to film from another angle. Meanwhile, no one cares too much whether or not spotlights or microphones are noticed, in the context of an atmosphere in which improvising setting and staging only adds to the legitimacy enjoyed by self-reflexivity. Television presents itself to us as a process of production rather than as final result alone.

If live recording gives the impression that there is no one standing between the image and its referent, or between image and viewing public, and that what can be seen on the screen is an outpouring of life itself, self-reflexivity would at first sight seem to produce the opposite effect. But on the contrary, in fact, self-reflexivity promises that the viewing public will (at least hypothetically) be able to see the same as what the technicians, directors, actors, and stars see. Nobody is manipulating what is being shown, because all manipulation can be shown and can be discussed. Television tells its story unaided, and as such *sincerely.* There is nothing up its sleeves; television claims to have clean hands. The unbridled use of special effects such as split screens, color modification, superimpositions, slow motion, or computerized effects, also characteristic of actually existing television, coexists with self-reflexivity without canceling it out. Perhaps this is one of the miracles of televisual rhetoric in recent years: It combines a "realism" that ensures the presence of "life" onscreen, constant allusion to how this "life" arrived there, and discursive operations that ensure that this "life" is attractive rather than simply sordid or banal.

Television wants us to be on its side. Here it differs from the cinema, which needs darkness, distance, silence, and careful concentration; television requires none of these situations or qualities. Self-reflexivity, which in literature is a mark of distance, functions in television as a *seal of proximity* that enables the play of complicities between television and its viewing public. Of all the discourses circulating in a given society, it is televisual discourse that produces the greatest effect of familiarity. Television's aura thrives not on distance but on everyday myths. There is only one way to learn how to watch television: by watching it. And it is undeniable that this learning process is cheap, antielitist, and egalitarian.

It follows then that television never runs into any cultural obstacles blocking the realization of its self-reflexive operations. Equally, citation (which in literature or painting always presents the difficult task of recognition) can be employed by television without misgivings: Every viewer trained in television is, in theory, sufficiently prepared to recognize its citations. Upon recognizing an allusion, viewers then experience a pleasure based on the cultural tie that links them to the medium. Television acknowledges us as television experts, and so provides us with those moments in which viewer knowledge is indispensable for meaning-construction. Moments like these arise when we need to know that a rival program is being referred to, when use is made of a set phrase invented on another program, when the plot of a commercial is mentioned, or when an interview with a star makes the assumption that we, the viewing public, know everything about what she or he does on television.

Citation leads in the end to parody, which these days is used as a fundamental strategy in television comedy. Every day, entire programs consist of parodies of other programs, from their titles, their characters' hairstyles, their ways of speaking, to their actors' tics; *they repeat their repetitions.* At the other extreme of the scale is imitation, which serves as the strategy of channels envious of a rival program's success. Imitation turns out to be a less interesting strategy, because its logic of reproduction with variation is inherently more a function of market competition than it is a matter of discursive forms.

Citation and parody, on the other hand, constitute surplus meaning. To unlock this surplus, you have first to be familiar with the cited discourse, and then to recognize it again in its new context. Both operations should be immediate because, like jokes, citation and parody lose all their effect once explained. Television lives off citing and parodying itself to the point at which the procedure's repetition comes to strip it of any critical significance. Televisual parody is simple. It operates by submitting well-known meanings to processes of distortion (caricature, exaggeration, or repetition). It establishes only a minimal distance (guaranteeing immediate recognition) between parody and parodied, regulated by a principle of repetition. Hence television has resurrected the impersonator, a breed of entertainer whose origin lies in theatrical reviews, and which was on the point of extinction. The uncertainty that parody induces in other discourses (such as the literary) is destroyed by the proximity between parody and parodied established by television.

The presence of these operations has often been advanced as proof of televisual discourse's relative formal sophistication. I would like to agree with this point of view, but I cannot. Television lives off citation more for reasons of intellectual laziness than anything else. It devours its own discourses, digests them, and offers them up again slightly altered by parodic distance, but not so altered that it would be difficult to recognize them, which might produce a moment in which meanings became indeterminate. This cultivation of citation and parody has more to do with television's mode of production than with any intention to be particularly critical. Because television is made quickly, it returns with exceptional frequency to what it already knows, and what television already knows is television. In countries where there is more time or money allocated to television production, television's self-citation and self-parody are strategies that do not appear with the frequency with which they are employed in countries where television has fewer resources or is greedier for quick and easy profits. Not so much a display of creative or critical daring, "hyper-parody" in fact represents a failure of the imagination needed to produce other forms of comedy, satire, stylization, or the absurd.

With parody and citation, television recycles itself and makes its own discourse its only discursive horizon, even when it deals with characters or meanings that originate outside the medium. In such cases, television takes this material as it appears on the screen, and then performs its operations of parodic distortion on this image. Television never takes for granted any existence outside television: Its citations from the extratelevisual are always already framed and preceded by a media image. Some may say that this trait reinforces television's inherent democratic impulses, by emphasizing the community established between medium and viewing public. Some may say that parodic recycling produces "deviant" or unstable readings, and "renegade meanings." As far as I am concerned, however, I would maintain that the opposite occurs. Out of all the infinite possibilities of quotation, parody, and recycling, television as we know it now works with the very lowest level of transformation, and it does this in order to avoid unduly obstructing viewer recognition of whatever discourse is cited, and hence to avoid undue risk to the comic or critical effect. In general, television limits itself to exaggerating the traits of what it parodies, displaying these traits in close-up, as it were. Basically, televisual parody magnifies things to the point of distortion without concerning itself with secondary details, and without producing any new configurations that would deviate from the original discourse. With television, any hesitation over the nature of an allusion is out of the question (except out of simple ignorance of earlier televisual material). You know immediately when there is imitation or parody; stylization, irony, or homage are generally ruled out. The limited range of these ways in which citation is used is not some inevitable destiny built into the medium itself; rather it is determined by a rhetoric that must perpetually and everywhere guarantee that it has kept open an escape route, that it has let down a rope by which all its viewers can descend rapidly to earth.

There has been much talk about the way in which television recycles genres. Even sophisticated critics have subscribed to this thesis and have promised to provide examples confirming it. In general, the examples offered are always the same: Discussion centers around commercials that recycle commercials or that imitate films, and around films that would show the influence of commercials (that, in turn, were earlier influenced by other films). When called upon for historical examples, everyone resorts to the handy nineteenth-century newspaper serial that is allegedly the soap opera's ancestor; the more ingenious look for old forms of popular comedy that television is supposed to have taken up again after a period of disuse. A serious approach to this discussion would demand that we distinguish the way in which the medium recycles its own forms (as in television's self-absorbed gaze made up of self-reflexivity and self-citation) from any recuperation of genres taken from literature, music, the circus, or anywhere else.

The case of literary genres presents a whole number of problems, among them that of the translation of a written discourse into one made up of sound and vision. It may be the case that television has done much more than simply recycling the serial novel (in which case its admirers fail to give it enough credit). But it has also done much less, limiting itself to reproducing a system of characters, maintaining a world in which value is determined by simple and symmetrical oppositions, and weakly threading together action by resorting to certain set plot devices. Again we see dramas of recognition in which forgotten, lost, or changed fathers, mothers, and children are discovered, typically at a point of crisis that is full of conflicts and that more often than not touches on the incest taboo. Once more we see how society impedes virtue, we see the notion of love's riches, and a couple of other themes besides. If this is the value of what television does with the serial novel, then there is no problem agreeing that it has efficiently dragged a genre (already taken up by the radio) from the nineteenth century to the present. Let us admit that television has done no disservice to the serial novel, that genre so scorned by intellectual elites because of their aesthetic and social prejudices.

The various defenses of television have already been repeated too often. But why limit its potential with this well-known mix of elegy and celebration of its charitable recuperation of forgotten genres? When done well, the television serial is all well and good. It is not so good (no matter how much recycling it may produce) when it fails to live up to the genre's minimal requirements, which include suspense, close interweavings of the personal and the social, plot complications that are unexpected without being completely unbelievable (because the serial novel, if it is the serial novel that is under discussion, is at least minimally realistic), and a combination of repetition to detain our interest plus novelty to maintain it. Yet there is still another possibility, one that the television with which I am familiar fails to fulfill: the possibility that television might produce new types of fiction that would go beyond the newspaper serial's basic schema.

Even so, it cannot be said that television is the only discourse that proposes to recycle traditional genres or to universalize parody as almost the only means to produce comedy. There is a delicate but fairly obvious network linking this televisual trait to extratelevisual forms, even to some projects deriving from circuits apparently far removed from television, such as underground youth theater.

A whole system of borrowings has arisen by which television feeds into the underground that, later, achieves some kind of recognition on television. Expressed in these terms, this circuit might seem almost ideal, something like an avant-garde invention working toward aesthetic republicanism. Still, whenever the underground takes a turn toward the televisual (in the most general terms, when it becomes particularly or exclusively parodic; or particularly or exclusively involved in dressing up traditional genres), it turns its most daring characteristics into a style that has found in parody the hegemonic resources of comedy, drama, and critique. Television interpellates this underground, improving the quality of its own production, and endorsing a circuit of mutual inspiration. Defenders of this circuit may invoke the inspiration that the avant-gardes found in the arts of cabaret, caricature, fairground comedy, packaging, or the cartoon strip. It seems to me, however, that the avant-gardes did not give up on their own distinctive features when they worked with these stylistic traits: They could accommodate everything within their own writing.

To take an especially problematic example, in which innovation comes closest to the market's methods and iconography, let us take a detour to examine pop art. Ever since pop, art's consumption of mass media symbols, trademarks, or icons has lost the capacity to shock. We know that anything can be material for aesthetics (and in a way this all began with modern art). What pop brought with it was the news (though it was not exactly the first time we had heard it) that art was dead, and subjectivity in terminal decline. Pop took unabashed joy in throwing itself into consumption, and chose common consumer items for its object—soup-cans, magazine photographs, films, Coca-Cola, shoes, soap boxes, and cartoon strips. It cast an aestheticizing eye over these tempting leftovers, and recomposed them through the use of series, enlargements, repetitions, exact copies, miniaturizations, and blowups. But even when it seems closest to the objects it takes up, pop exercises at least some degree of symbolic violence against them. Copying a soup-can down to the smallest detail is not the same as parodying a soup-can's design. Though it may seem otherwise, an exact copy presents more aesthetic problems than does distortion, because it forcefully challenges the idea that art transforms everything it touches, and that the artist is defined by the personal stamp she or he leaves even on the most banal of objects. The exact copy is, in its own exactitude, ironic.

Pop is impossible without this double distance that, on the one hand, is a critique of consecrated art originating in a tendency of this century's avant-gardes and that, on the other hand, changes the uses available for a soup-can or a comic strip frame to say "this is what can be done with that." Pop was consumerist and celebratory, a huge recycling and mixing machine, but it kept the distance that made the pop operation, precisely, possible. Though its aesthetic legacy is less interesting than that of the avant-gardes that preceded it, we need to recognize that pop takes to its limit the affirmation that artistic materials are indifferent. In brief: After pop, nobody could be scandalized (or surprised) by any recycling.

When the underground is seduced by the mass media, the bolero, and magazines, it resorts to a path few today would contest, and opens doors that, in fact, have been open ever since sixties pop art left them so. But it opens these doors for a young public that has surely never gone through pop's worldly aesthetic scandals. The underground's aesthetic program is in fact more moderate than are its libertarian ideas about sexuality, violence, religion, traditional authorities, and transvestitism, all fields in which it chooses bold themes and achieves effects that are "progressive" (however unpopular this adjective may be today).

This is probably why the media industry (which, believe it or not, has always known that you should worry more about the form than the content of ideas) can incorporate fairly peaceably the parody offered it by the underground. Like nineteenth-century white imperialism, television has no respect for borders: Therein lies its strength.

Chapter 3

Popular Cultures, Old and New

Once, in a little mountain town, I heard the following story, as told by its protagonist: "Three nights ago I had a tall, chestnut stallion stolen from me—not the one I always bring here, but the other, a big horse more than five feet in height or near enough. I had lent him to my brother-in-law, who hadn't any horses left because he'd sold his to roof his house—you know, the one that's on the crest of the hill just before you get to the highway and the tennis courts. My brother-in-law doesn't have good dogs, so the horse was there just tied with a chain. They took the horse and left the chain. That's why you haven't seen me the past day or two: We went out looking for him because a friend told me he was sure that the horse had been taken by a band from the other side of the hills, who do these things out of pure wickedness. They steal horses and ride them for a while and then sell them if they can, but on the whole they don't sell them, because they're little more than mischief makers—though this is serious mischief—and what's more they'd have to go a fair way away to sell this stallion because anyone around here would recognize one of my horses.

"We looked for him all day, and then I came back home in the evening. I was just unsaddling when my friend turns up, along with my brother-in-law, who had already started heading home when my friend stopped him on the road. 'They've spotted your horse,' he tells me, 'near the dam.' Now, I didn't go off to inform the police about this because they don't do anything but fill out forms. So I saddled up again and we set off with my dogs, which are pretty good trackers; and there was the stallion, bruised all over, in a field right by the river-bank, just before the dam, just like my friend had been told. No doubt they'd made him push against some wire fence or made him run in some kind of race—they're just wicked. His bruises weren't too bad, but his shoulder blade was injured and he was missing a shoe, and I had shoed him only the week before.

"Later on, yesterday afternoon, my friend came back and told me, 'The other afternoon your horse was seen at a party— a big party, something to do with a wedding—in the village on the other side of the dam. The person who saw this thought that you'd lent the horse to them, because they rode him in the procession that went to the church as well as at the party later.' Obviously they abandoned the horse after the dance was over, when they were drunk and couldn't ride it anymore. My friend tells me, 'They promised me they'd get you the video of the party; it'll be easy to spot your horse.' So now I'm waiting for the video, so I can identify the culprit. The police won't be able to tell me that they have no idea who stole the horse and that therefore it's not worth looking for them. The guy my friend knows promised to bring the video this after-noon. I want them to pay me the price of the horse's rental, two whole days' worth, and that of the other horses used in the search, as well as what the poor animal's injuries will cost me—who knows how he comes out in the video? You've seen that he's a pretty distinctive horse, but it was only fifteen days ago that I'd shorn him. The boys from the cable company told me they'd show the video on the local TV news, so that people can be on their guard against these thieves. Later, don't be sur-prised if you see me sell the horse, because it's going to be fa-mous. I'm sure I'll get a good price."

It has been said that popular cultures come to seem interest-ing only the moment they start to disappear. Anthropologists, historians, sociologists, and critics study something that now hardly exists the way it existed in the not too distant past: Rural peasant cultures have vanished, or uncontaminated rural cultures at least, except in very poorest areas where capitalism has confined itself to subsistence and destruction. Urban cultures are a dynamic mixture, a space swept by the winds of the mass media. What was once, in some countries, working-class culture has been eroded by transformations in the system of production, by a new type of unionism, by unemployment, by the conversion of thousands of workers into service employees, and, of course, by the common denominator that is the communications media. Popular cultures are an artifact that no longer exists in a state of purity.

Hybridization, mestizaje, recycling, and *mixture* are the words used to describe this phenomenon. Popular sectors no longer live confined to the physical space of neighborhood, slum, or factory. On the roofs of houses, on the muddy slopes occupied by slums, along village alleyways, and on deteriorating apartment blocks, television antennae extend imaginary lines making for a new cultural cartography. The hermeticism of rural peasant cultures, including the misery and isolation of indigenous communities, has been breached: The indigenous have been quick to learn that if they want to be heard in the city, they have to use the same media through which they themselves hear what is going on in the city. Dressed in their traditional costumes modernized with the use of nylon and jeans, with sneakers on their feet and plastic bags protecting their hats, they demonstrate in the public square but call on the television to make sure their demonstration is seen. We have to reject any notion that would assimilate what is going on now to what happened in the past: While it is certainly true that it would be difficult to point to a time when popular cultures existed in absolutely closed universes, the speed and reach of what is happening now is unprecedented.

Popular cultures no longer listen to traditional authorities (the Church or those dominant sectors most in touch with the world of the popular, such as old-style intellectuals, paternalistic politicians, caudillos, or semifeudal bosses) as though they were some privileged voice from outside. The fact that cracks have opened up in traditions has had a liberating, democratizing, and secularizing effect regarding outmoded authorities and cultural traits. Priests and aristocrats had first to compete with unions, with the school, and with politicians; today all these sources of authority have to compete with each other and with the mass media. The Church is worried about electronic evangelists, whose reach is further than that of their own ministers, and about the sects, which operate with televisual style and appeal. Traditional politicians are worried about the increasing skepticism that greets their words in communities where they used to lay down the law, a skepticism that arises when the media let people hear other words and see other faces. The school, materially and symbolically impoverished, does not know how to make what it has to offer seem more attractive than media culture.

Beliefs, knowledges, and loyalties are all affected by the reach of the mass media. The arrival of a technological revolution of the magnitude implied by the electronic transmission of images and sounds reconfigures every level of culture. Nowadays there is no need to wait for the visit of a caudillo, priest, or pamphlet vendor for news of the city to make its way to the countryside; the city is always there. City time and the time of rural peasant space, once separated by distances bridged weekly by the railroad, newspaper, and books, are now synchronized. And within the city itself, the mass media's lymphatic system conveys the same sense of time to rich and poor, unemployed and jet set, old and young. National unity is as dependent upon media communication as it once was upon the mail system, the railroads, or the school. With the arrival of television, all subcultures share a spatial continuum that is both national and international but that takes on local characteristics in line with the strength of each country's cultural industries. This situation used to be a source of concern for old-style populists, but it does not worry the market neopopulists who find in each local use of international or national styles irrefutable proof of the unending palimpsest written by popular sectors using materials that reach them over the air. My friend who thought he could catch a horse thief by identifying him in the right video tape is the ideal hero for a neopopulist epic.

Even so, a world in which independence and symbolic equality reign has yet to arrive. The mass media undermine old powers, but have hardly the will or the ability to lay the foundations upon which to construct new, autonomous powers. It is like the story of the gardener's dog that stopped its old master from eating but at the same time could not stand anyone preparing their own food. Now whatever our particular diet, at root what we consume has been prepared by the media. As a result, popular cultures are in the middle of a long transition and it is hard to draw up a balance sheet of what this transition implies. We know what has been lost, but no one can be so sure of what has been gained with the advent of the communications media's hegemony. On the side of what has been lost one has to include crystallized identities and old prejudices. Today we are accustomed to condemn attitudes (such as machismo or domestic violence) that once seemed to be just part of the way things naturally were. We should also reckon that blind obedience to traditional forms of symbolic authority (caudillo, landlord, priest, father, or teacher) has also been lost. As can be seen even in making this list, not every instance of obedience had the same consequences for those who obeyed. We need only point out that the school, for one, was once an essential element in a liberating modernization for popular sectors who knew from the start the value of knowledge, and who managed to take advantage of the school, freeing themselves from the deterministic double bind that turns every transmission of knowledge into the imposition of power. The fact that the school is now so weak, and that it is unable to distribute basic knowledges in a minimally acceptable manner, is one of the worst obstacles to the construction of a common culture that would not be supported solely by the imaginary community produced by the mass media.

We also see a lack of coordination among the powers set

free by the transformation of traditional popular identities—
transformed after modernization processes wore away their
most prominent characteristics. Media culture turns us all into
members of an electronic society that is presented to the imagination as a society of equals. At first sight there is nothing
more democratic than the electronic culture whose need for
ratings obliges it to assimilate, seamlessly, cultural fragments
from the most diverse of sources. We can all feel that there is
something of us in the media and, at the same time, we can
all fantasize that we can appropriate and make use of what
the media offer us. Everyone—the destitute, the marginalized,
those who are simply poor, workers and the unemployed, city
dwellers and peasants—finds in the media a culture that seems
to fit comfortably and, we are led to believe, offers to satisfy
our tastes and desires. This imaginary consumption (imaginary in all senses of the word) reorganizes the ways in which
popular sectors relate to their own experience, to politics, to
language, to the market, and to conceptions of ideal beauty
and health. In other words, it reorganizes everything that
shapes social identity.

Traditional identities were stable over the long term and
subject to centripetal forces that operated as much on their
original traits as on the elements and values imposed by economic and symbolic domination. Today identities are going
through processes of "balkanization." Such identities attempt
to survive in a contemporary world destabilized by the disappearance of traditional certainties and by the erosion of memory; their transformation points to the breakdown of accepted
norms, while their weakness underlines the way in which common values and goals are now empty. Village solidarity was
once close even as it was also, often, egotistical, violent, sexist,
and merciless to those who were different. This network of
face-to-face bonds, through which premodern principles of
cohesion founded strong communities based in traditional authorities, is now irreversibly shattered. The old strategies can
no longer suture the divisions arising from new differences.

Many communities have lost their territorial character.

Migrations take men and women to unfamiliar environments where their cultural ties, even if they can be reintroduced, conflict with what remains of other communities or with new elements from urban cultures. In such situations the big communications media act like the most corrosive of acids upon traditional loyalties and certainties. But the media also bridge the remains of old worlds once separated by cultural distance and space, producing a new type of globalism. Paradoxically, the era of individualism we live in flourishes on the terrain of the most inclusive of electronic communities. Yet the cracks that once separated distinct cultural communities have yet to close up fully, because in some cases those old cultures were too powerful to disappear altogether. Moreover, and fundamentally, economic differences and social obstacles that lie between us and a truly universal use of symbolic goods persist with all the tenacity of the material. Still, the strength of old identities has been toned down and, though it is true that the last word has yet to be said and that there are times when the old symbols are used once more in new cultural or geographical contexts, above all such identities have lost their ability to arouse feelings of belonging.

Even those sectors that are for the most part settled in a single location have been deterritorialized: Today neighborhoods, sites of association where experience and face-to-face relationships are built, do not have the importance they had forty or fifty years ago. In many cities, working-class neighborhoods and local municipalities are unsafe areas where everyday violence constitutes an argument for private withdrawal. And at the center of the private sphere gleams the small screen, always on. The neighborhood has stopped being a territory of use and belonging because its inhabitants have taken part in the contradictory double process of opening themselves up beyond any border, converting themselves into the media's viewing public, and staying evermore within their own homes. Those places that were formerly and traditionally centers of interaction—such as the school, public libraries, political committees, lobbying groups, or neighborhood clubs—are no longer what they once were, when they were places where identity's contours and community feeling were defined. These places, in which the culture of the written word and individual, face-to-face relations are still dominant, today interpellate people much less than they did. We no longer resort to them on an everyday basis, only at moments of crisis or pressing need.

The youngest members of society today do not find here any of the cultural traits that once attracted young people to these spaces forty or fifty years ago. And without young people, any hope of cultural transmission is doomed. Other spaces offer alternatives more in tune with the qualities of media culture. These include churches whose style is inspired in electronic ministry; organizations that focus on short-term objectives guaranteed not to contaminate anyone with politics, and to encourage democratic horizontalism and a minimum of institutional structure; video game arcades; nightclubs that cater to the subtlest of niche publics, segregating their clientele with resolute self-consciousness; and fan clubs whose membership originates in media culture (though there are exceptions as some rock bands have been able to establish connections that do not depend upon the mass media; in any case, the media have become expert at not letting a phenomenon escape them completely even if it might have passed them by initially).

Today youth culture is a dynamic facet—perhaps the most dynamic—of all cultures, be they popular or elite. However discerning young people's eye for all networks of distinction may be, youth culture tends to be universal and in fact crosses class and national barriers. Cultural experiences are divided up according to the pyramid of ages more fundamentally than by any other social groupings. There are still differences within youth culture (which in rock culture are the basis of a real tribalism), but the force of universalization carries more weight than either old subcultural particularisms or new modes of discrimination.

The only effective obstacle to cultural homogenization is economic inequality: Everyone's desires are becoming more similar, but not everyone's desires have the same chances of realization. Ideology constitutes us as universal consumers without regard for the fact that there are millions who are only imaginary consumers. If in the past belonging to a culture ensured the possession of symbolic goods that constituted the basis for strong identities, today consumerism's exclusiveness makes all identities unstable. It is precisely in youth culture that it is most evident that desiring a manufacturer's label manufactures social labels.

There have been winners and losers. Among the losers are the lettered elite who once held a monopoly on cultural legitimacy, for which only the elite's various fractions could contend. Now all the various elite fractions find themselves confronted with new mechanisms through which legitimacy is produced today; they can no longer legislate about taste with their accustomed haughty independence because there are other centers of legitimation dictating the way things should be. Media culture elects its own judges and recognizes power in numbers now that its business is the incessant expansion of audiences rather than an elitist distinction between fractions. The phenomenon of differentiation between subcultures is subordinate to the processes of expansion and homogenization. While cultural neotribalism gives one the feeling that the most exclusive particularisms can be cultivated with absolute liberty, these particularisms are allowed to stand uncontradicted only so long as they are not in contention with each other in the context of the global media market. When they do begin to contend with each other, as has happened in many places with FM radio stations, the good and the great of the cultural industry first kick up an almighty fuss and then think up new strategies to intervene in this new market predicated upon the almost infinite fractionalization of the radio dial.

A new type of subordination underlies the accentuation of these particularisms. It is not the dominant classes (with their complicated system of institutions and delegations) that construct articulations bridging the limits between social fractions. As a result it is no longer possible to speak either of a cultural hegemony of the dominant classes or of measuring cultural autonomy only in terms of distance from the culture imposed by elites. Today the likely outcome for any independent cultural initiative is determined wholly by the particular form in which different social groups are prepared to integrate their own cultural resources with those of lettered culture and those of the communications media. Depending on the relations between these three dimensions (elements proper to the initiative's own identity, institutional culture propagated by the school, and media culture), differing and unstable configurations are produced that can change according to the political conjuncture or social climate. Within the framework of media hegemony, some especially clear-cut situations (such as the passage from dictatorship to democracy) reroute the channels through which this hegemony is exercised. These are particular episodes in which values are reordered and habitual patterns of behavior broken, on the basis of a mix of elements originating in cultural tradition, in institutional culture, in new political articulations, and in the mass media. Often, and this is quite evident during elections, media discourse is short-circuited when it comes into contact with deep-rooted political identities or new ideals that the media (out of censorship or blindness) has not encouraged. At these moments subcultures go through phases of relatively independent restructuring, even if they do not always persist after the particular conjuncture has exhausted its ideological potential.

Whatever the case, if once-popular cultures had strong and clearly demarcated limits, these limits have now become blurred. Likewise the more durable characteristics that once distinguished powerful elites have faded. Material consumption's imaginary universalism and media networks' total coverage of physical space do not put an end to social differences, but they do dilute some of the outward manifestations that depend upon these differences. The case of spoken language is particularly significant. For decades, speaking language "correctly" was one of the school's ideals; now the school is not in a position to transmit any ideal whatsoever. On the other hand, linguistic life and creativity run their course far removed from lettered culture while linguistic homogenization smooths over regional, class, or occupational differences. This leveling impulse resonates with something like democratization, especially if it is compared with the hyperstratified language of some European countries. And yet not everything can be put under the heading of democratic leveling when a president or a parliamentarian's discourse is the source of the most characteristic examples of popular language. It is useless to search for the origin of the circle by which politicians speak like soccer players or like television floozies, doing so to imitate the latter's success, thus courting neopopulism, or (it is also said) to get near to the people, who are turned thus into a community of viewers, rather than citizens, who would then reciprocally consecrate the politicians according to criteria defined by media aura.

Everyone speaks the same way and linguistic innovation migrates at great speed from one social fraction to another. Though it may be true that strong lexical and phonetic traits are retained by traditional sectors of the old elites, nonetheless these strata have more in common with the rest of society than they have differentiating them. Even though people themselves may hold on to the system of distinction between class fractions as though it were a protecting shield, such distinction is now attenuated because it is less and less founded in cultural elements that are inaccessible to the majority, as it rests rather on elements that are within everyone's reach. Being distinguished for fluently speaking a foreign language is not the same as being distinguished for having bought the latest Guns N' Roses compact disc. Having a Japanese motorbike does not produce the same kind of unattainable distinction as does access to a family library: One could imagine at least that anyone could buy a Japanese motorbike. The market's symbolism, equally accessible to all, tends to cancel out symbolism pertaining to the old regime of domination based upon difference and upon setting unsurpassable limits.

What was once considered lettered culture (the only legitimate culture, at least for the lettered elite itself) no longer organizes the hierarchy of cultures and subcultures. In the face of this, the lettered elite opts for one of two possible attitudes. Some lament the fact that the values on which their lettered hegemony was based have now been shipwrecked. Others celebrate the fact that the remains of the shipwreck have reached the shore, and they use this flotsam to outfit some new contraption that is to analyze the new subcultures and the popular uses of what the media leave behind. Those taking the first option distrust what the present promises; the market neopopulists taking the second option believe these promises fervently. The former group are partisans of the old mode of legitimation in that they still respect a cultural hierarchy in which the culture of the written word was secure in its hegemonic position, anchoring the pretensions of other cultural forms. Those in the second group are partisans of the new mode of legitimation because, from within the shipwreck of the culture of the written word and high culture, they ensconce their own power to decode and interpret what the people do with the remains of their own culture and fragments seized from the culture of the mass media. Here everything has been permanently turned upside down: Neopopulists recognize only one mode of legitimation, that of the cultures formed at the crossroads of experience and media discourse. They consider the limits placed on high culture to constitute a symbolic revolution, in which those who were once downtrodden can make themselves masters of their own fate by means of a craftsmanlike use of zapping and other technological resources taken from media culture.

The confrontation between these two positions can be summed up in terms that were popular almost thirty years ago: Those prophesying apocalypse (whom we would today call partisans of the old mode of legitimation, unyielding in their defense of the way culture was before its media reorganization) face the advocates of integration (the unpaid or self-elected defenders of the media industries and their new mode of cultural legitimation).

Still, some issues stubbornly refuse to go away. To begin with, there is the problem of unequal access to symbolic goods. This inequality is far from weakening, and rather is growing now that the school system is undergoing an economic crisis whose flip side is also a crisis over what its aims should be, combined with an erosion of the school's authority and the lack of new forms of direction to replace it. In the early part of this century, schools benefited from the fact that popular and elite sectors alike saw them as bathed in the luster of prestige; this is no longer the case. In most Latin American countries, the public school is today the site of symbolic poverty. Here teachers, curricula, and their resources compete against mass media that have almost complete coverage of the national territory and to which access is either free or relatively inexpensive. In these conditions the school's defeat is almost certain.

We know that lettered culture is in crisis worldwide: U.S. administrators look on with envy at the exam results achieved by Japanese children who in turn are submitted to samurai discipline to prevent any fall in their performance. In the French school system, too, they bewail declining standards, above all in the humanities, and in the past ten years they have aimed two programs for reform, one after another, at a system already reformed in the heat of the sixties anti-institutional atmosphere. Examples abound of ever more delayed and less complete mastery of basic skills: We are seeing a crisis of literacy (and hence of the culture of the written word) while mass media optimists celebrate the skills acquired in zapping and in playing video games. Let us just point out quickly that the source of this crisis is not simply the expansion of schooling to previously unincorporated social sectors (migrants, ethnic minorities, and so on); in fact, in recent years and in countries in which the expansion to universal schooling took place decades ago, the crisis has come about independently of whatever effects may have arisen from the inclusion of racial or religious minorities, or from the partial inclusion of the most dispossessed. The literacy crisis affects children of the urban middle classes, of workers involved in skilled manual labor, and the petite bourgeoisie. This is an issue of special importance in Latin America, where everyday problems build up within the framework of weak institutions made ever weaker by economic adjustment programs and a shrinking State.

It is said that schools were unprepared for mass media culture's arrival. Neither educational programs nor educational bureaucracies have been updated at a speed that would keep up with the transformations that have affected society over the last thirty years. All this is true. But it is not only a question of material conditions or equipment—the richest schools in the private sector can deal with such necessities and, in many cases, find it no problem to provide them. By contrast, for the poorest schools (and there are thousands of them) in any Latin American country, the need to buy a television, VCR, or computer can represent an impossible obstacle. Yet in any case, even supposing that Sony and IBM were to decide to practice some kind of philanthropy on a giant scale, even so, the problem I wish to outline would remain in place precisely because what is at issue is not simply a question of technical equipment but is rather a matter of the way in which culture itself has changed.

Schools (it is said) could benefit and increase their efficiency by making new use of the skills their pupils have learned elsewhere: skills such as the feeling for speed acquired by playing video games; the ability to take things in and respond when faced with a set of superimposed messages; or they could make new use of the content, both familiar and exotic, provided by the media. It would be absurd to argue that this is not the case, and yet we should still be able to ask whether or not these skills and knowledges are enough. We should ask whether or not we can regard them as tools that really aid in the acquisition of other knowledges even today still linked to the word, and to the logical or abstract mathematical processes of reasoning, the linguistic invention and argumentation that are, and will be for the foreseeable future, indispensable in the worlds of work, technology, and politics.

Neither the speed-reading cultivated by watching videos nor the light touch required for video games train those who have such skills in the intellectual capacities required to sit down and concentrate on a point on the screen of the simplest computer as is required, we all know, to solve the simplest of problems arising from use of the simplest of computer programs. They prepare far less for the management of much more sophisticated programs, such as Hypertext, that soon will be relatively accessible. Taking on board the applied information technology required in learning any discipline requires skills never used in playing Nintendo. It requires being able to read complex hierarchized syntaxes in conditions of less speed, less trust of motor reflexes, less impatience, of results that are very much deferred. It involves a whole narrative of success, trial, and error that is opposed to the speed of the results provided by video clips and video games however much it may be true that games operators have a closer and bolder relationship with the machine than their parents and teachers have. Learning of this sort involves working with a limited number of semantic and logical elements in any given period of time or, in other words, an ability to read intensively. True learning is a process that involves setting distances, incorporating differences, exploring the unknown, in which what is learned first are learning skills themselves and what we could call learning's necessary psycho-moral conditions of possibility.

Acquiring a common culture—a democratic ideal that could do with some reinvention, in the direction of greater pluralism and respect for difference, but which should not be thrown out altogether—presupposes a series of processes breaking with and not simply continuing on from the everyday. As a result, you gain an appreciation of what you don't know: This simple idea forces you to consider others. Above all, it forces you to consider that your symbolic inheritance lies not only in what has come to you and what you consider yours already (culture acquired through lived experience in your own family, ethnic group, or society) but also in what you come to make your own through a process that implies, even in the moment of appropriation, a certain difficulty and distance.

Sony's hypothetical donation to Latin America's poorest schools would not alter the hard truth that it is a leap from "spontaneous" video culture to other cultural dimensions that is required. Nor would it alter the fact that even if it were to facilitate this leap while incorporating the media's technical and ludic dimensions, there would still be the need for a forceful initiative based on something other than social subjects' spontaneity. The kinds of training that children receive as spectators of Xuxa, the popular children's television show, or as video game players can only be used by the school up to a certain and very preliminary point. Beyond that point, the task is to convert Xuxa spectators into book readers, and any printed page, however simple, requires skills absent from the world according to Xuxa.

On the other hand, and despite some filmic fantasies that think that feminism consists of presenting girls who can operate a computer more skillfully than their little brothers, the fact is that for long-standing cultural reasons a video game player or computing aficionado is notoriously more likely to be a boy rather than a girl. This is true above all among popular sectors (who have neither computers nor game machines in the family): Thus in every large Latin American city an overwhelmingly male clientele frequents the video arcades. The universal reach of this skill acquisition is therefore not so very universal (at best it is only semiuniversal), and this fact might give pause for thought to technological optimists. Before celebrating the prospect of Sony's donation to all Latin America's run-down schools, it would be worth developing strategies to compensate for the distribution of skills between the sexes that, following the way of the market, shows a pronounced division in terms of sexual inequality.

Sony's donation would be as useless as an old 8 mm projector if schools used it only as an extension of game playing, trying to convince their pupils that learning is as much fun as watching television. Children, who are no fools, sense that this is untrue.

For a century or so the school has been a point of reference for the popular cultures of countries such as ours. Those who see the school as nothing more than an instrument of domination are wrong. Schools provided resources that became an active part of popular cultures' characteristics. Literacy permitted expanded diffusion of modern journalism from the beginning of the twentieth century onward, and in the first four decades of this century led to an enormously powerful mass publishing industry's blossoming and putting out hundreds of thousands of volumes of literature, high quality scientific popularization, history, drama, and poetry. Urban popular cultures did not disavow this contamination by lettered culture. Far from it, they adopted high-cultural elements that then played a leading role in the process of modernization and founded aspects of a common culture. Thousands of women from the middle and lower social sectors found the teaching profession to be a path to labor independence and the basis for a form of power that enabled relative autonomy from male authority. The school was a place that was symbolically rich and socially prestigious. Though there is no doubt that the school was one setting for symbolic domination, the school was not simply an institution of domination: It distributed knowledges and skills that the poor could not attain elsewhere.

It is true that schools destroyed some very rich cultural characteristics. Immigrants sent their children to school where they lost their parents' language and culture and found only the new language of their new country. But at the same time, this imposition turned these children into citizens rather than members of ethnic ghettos in which cultural differences would stay untouched along with inequalities between nationals and foreigners, between members of different religions and different ethnicities. The school scrubbed everything with its iron brush, but on top of its brutal conversion of immigrant cultures into blank slates it also furnished immigrant children with knowledges that were indispensable not only in their conversion into a capitalist labor force but also in founding those expressions of working-class culture that made use of the written word, such as unionization and interventions in political struggle.

The lettered elite imposed values, myths, historical narratives, and traditions upon popular sectors, all through a strong and interventionist school system. But the school system was also a secular space that was free and theoretically egalitarian, in which popular sectors seized hold of cultural resources that they then used for their own ends and interests. It is true that schools did not teach people to fight against symbolic domination, but it is also true that it provided tools with which they could affirm popular culture on a new basis, more varied and more modern than that provided by everyday experience and traditional knowledges. Building upon this distribution of cultural goods and skills, popular sectors carried out often very successful processes of adaptation and readjustment. Women, especially, found out early on about the legal equality that demanded their presence as much as men's in the schools.

The school was the setting for an extremely important chapter in the history of the operations through which popular sectors (together with the rest of society) today achieve forms of hybridization between popular cultures and media culture. It was in the school that, from the beginning of the twentieth century, people gained the necessary skills for them to become the great modern newspapers' readership, to understand technological transformations and master their technical elements, and to appropriate the knowledges that permitted independent uses of institutional objectives. By acquiring previously unfamiliar forms of knowledge that did not "naturally" belong to their immediate world, popular sectors did not so much adapt like robots to the contents of dominant culture, as much as they cut, pasted, sewed, fragmented, and recycled these contents. Yet industrial capitalism's culture is no compensation for the public school system's decline.

There are no uncontaminated cultures, or any cultures contaminated only by elite domination, and only the old-style populists could ever believe in the hypothetical "purity" of popular cultures. As a result, the question of popular cultures and their always relative autonomy must touch on the elements that enter into each moment of the mix. Everything depends upon the operations that popular sectors are able to carry out by building upon the cultural mix—a mix that is inevitable and that only a backward-looking and traditionalist perspective could stigmatize. Nobody can be blamed for the loss of an original purity that popular cultures have never, from modernity's outset, ever had.

As a result, there is no ideal paradigm in the past to which popular culture can be referred: Restoring authenticity is impossible and would only produce exhibitions of folkloric kitsch that would bore even its own protagonists. Just as written cultures return to their classics only by means of processes of transformation, defamiliarization, and irony, likewise popular cultures can view their origins solely from their present. In any case, assumptions about these origins lead to a complication from the start: When was the moment of true autonomy for a culture already permeated by modernity? Any such moment would be an ethnographic utopia visible only when staged by a museum. Luckily, popular sectors have no time for this ethnographic calling and make whatever they can of their past.

Yes, the conditions determining what they can do with their past may change and depend upon cultural policies over which popular sectors have very little say. Market neopopulists, dazzled by the encounter between the popular cultures' remnants and the mass media, close their eyes to evidence of unequal access to symbolic goods and as a result prefer not to mention economic and cultural domination. These neopopulists see the only worrying cultural imposition to be that of the lettered elites' holding on to a pedagogical paradigm opposed to laissez faire and their continuing, moreover, to maintain that the culture of the written word is fundamental within culture's contemporary configuration. On every other issue, in other words on the most important issues, the neopopulists have nothing to say.

And the most important issue concerns, precisely, the threads with which the mass media complete popular cultures' tattered tapestry. A cultural perspective that claims to be democratic and egalitarian ought to have something to say about this. So

long as the capitalist market remains in charge of cultural policy, the processes of hybridization among old traditions, everyday experiences, ever more complex new knowledges, and
media products will find that the market constitutes their true
planning ministry. This symbolic market underscores every inequality: unequal access to the institution of education; unequal abilities to choose within what the media offers; inequalities in inherited cultural formations. Popular sectors have no
all-powerful resource to compensate for what a school system
in crisis can no longer provide, for what the lettered elite can
acquire at leisure and at hardly any cost, or for those media
market goods that are either not free or not adapted to the
taste that the market protects precisely because it is the taste
that is most beneficial to its standardized products (and that
these very products have helped to form).

The cultural spontaneity of the popular sectors is no more
subversive, nationalist, or wise than that of other social factions. Old-style populists (the forebears of today's market
neopopulists) used to believe that they could find the cultural
reserves of national identity within the people. They attributed
to popular sectors what they, as populist intellectuals, were out
to find. Today we know that no lettered elite has the right to
ask others to concoct the popular or national essence that that
same elite requires to imagine itself at the head of a national
popular State. We know that these embodiments of the "national popular" can provide the foundation for proud independent identities, but they can also often take on the most hor-
rible faces of nationalism, racism, sexism, and fundamentalism.

We know then that just as there is no single legitimate culture, in whose book all should learn the same lesson, nor is
there any popular culture so wise and so powerful that it
might beat the mass media at every cultural game, constructing some free and proud collage out of the mass media's products registering only its own meaning while erasing the meanings and ideas that are dominant in the media themselves.
Nobody can pull off such a contestatory feat in his or her leisure time, while watching television.

The popular sectors have no more obligations than do the

lettered elites: It is not fair to expect them to be any more as-
tute, any more rebellious, any more persistent, to see things
any more clearly, or to represent anything or anyone other
than themselves. Yet what does differentiate them from the
economic and intellectual elites is that they have fewer material and symbolic possessions, worse conditions for making use
of culture, and fewer possibilities to exercise choices that
would not be conditioned either by the poverty of what is on
offer or by the scarcity of material and intellectual resources.
It is also the case that often they have more racial, sexual, or
national prejudices than do the intellectuals who have learned
to hide or do away with such prejudices. Hence they are neither bearers of truth nor responsible for revealing truth to the
world. They are simply social subjects who are part of a world
of material and symbolic differences.

Therefore if what is wanted is to create the conditions for
the free expression of all a society's different cultural levels, the
first of these conditions would be to guarantee democratic access to the storehouses holding the necessary tools. This means
a strong school system and greater possibilities of choosing
from different audiovisual offerings that might pose a challenge to what is offered by the capitalist media outlets, all of
which are as undifferentiated as are the commodities they produce. We could call what people might make with these resources hybridization, mixing, or whatever. The key point is
that, if hybridization is to be an effective form of cultural construction, the material that goes into its cauldron should be
chosen by the freest means possible and by means that are more
egalitarian from an institutional and economic point of view.

The other option on offer, the indiscriminate celebration of
strategies of popular survival within the mass media's continu-
al flow, implies not so much putting one's trust in the people's
initiative and originality, as handing everything over to the
way in which social differences specific to capitalism express
themselves and believing—and now this indeed is in the style
of classical populism—that everything the people does is wise
and perfectly in line with their own interests.

Chapter 4

The Place of Art

Let us agree on something. Never, since printing's invention, have so many books or so many newspapers and magazines been published each year. It is also true that, except in cases of exceptional blindness (such as our unfortunate situation in Argentina), television and radio do pay attention to writers and artists. Are we then in the best of all possible worlds?

It would be hard to give an unequivocal answer to this question. The culture industry (made up of the cinema, television, the recording industry, promoters, and publishing houses) has more economic power than the founders of an empire such as Hollywood could ever have dared to dream. And yet, taking the cinema as an example, we see events there illustrating in spectacular manner the knotted set of problems whose threads nowadays tie audiences, artists, and capitalist investors to one another.

I would begin with a question about the cinema whose virtue is its general interest. Why would a new Yasujiro Ozu or John Ford be unthinkable today? These were film directors firmly rooted in the culture industry, Ozu as much as Ford, who had a dedicated mass following and at the same time produced a style truly their own. They take their place in the ranks of the twentieth century's great directors alongside those who had less public success and who were more programmatically linked to arthouse film. You could never say of them, as you could of the avant-gardes, that they worked against the grain of the audience's common sense. Nor could you say that their art is pure negativity, an aesthetic critique turned to ideology critique. Quite the opposite, Ozu's and Ford's cinematographic success not only kept them squarely within the culture industry, but also made them crucial to financing a mass cinema in the 1930s and 1940s. The major studios did not simply churn out banalities for viewing on the world's cinema screens; with the films of Ozu and Ford (or Wyler, or before that Griffiths and Chaplin, or, if we get down to it, Hitchcock), they were also responsible for works of perfection in which cinematic language is developed to the point at which it reaches its classic state. These films are perfectly recognizable: Ford's wide shots and Ozu's framing are today considered marks of their personal style that have now become part of the cinema's grammar.

There is an endless series of possible questions along the lines of the one concerning Ozu and Ford. For example, what gives us the conviction that *Fame* or *Saturday Night Fever* are so far removed from *Singing in the Rain*? Stanley Donen and Gene Kelly's film was an immediate and huge success at the same time as it was a model musical whose obsession with detail made for its impeccable form. What made the work of these directors and these films both outstanding aesthetic achievements and, at the same time, huge favorites with all types of audience?

Perhaps the question is poorly put. The right formulation would probably be the following: What allowed Ford and Ozu, or Hitchcock and Wyler, to be understood by a mass audience that appreciated *Rio Grande* or *Tokyo Story* as much as it lapped up the most banal of cinematic productions? What can we say about this audience's culture? What conditions operated to ensure that Ozu and Ford were not simply tolerated on the margins, but rather were positioned at the center of a whole system of production and commercial consecration (one in Japan, the other in the United States)?

Part of the answer is that the culture industry had not yet fully established its hegemony over all previous cultural forms.

Another part is that the avant-gardes had not yet completely made a definitive break with the field of art. Once these two things happened, in the mid-twentieth century, audience expansion (and stratification) and aesthetic experimentation took divergent paths that have ever since intersected in only a small number of very exceptional cases. This split replicated what had already occurred earlier with music and literature.

Why worry about a process that seems irreversible and what is more, has palpably democratic aspects? In effect, the culture industry's establishment can bring about greater equality, and it sets up an iron framework for what many are pleased to call a "common culture." Nobody would want to distance him- or herself from such optimism, much less offer an elitist critique of such processes.

Yet the pages that follow will try, through a series of portraits of writers and painters, to trace those typically modern characteristics that pertain to art but that seem destined, thanks to market media culture, to inhabit an attic visited only by specialists or by audiences whose motivation is very much tied to their careers. The model of the artist presented in these portraits is palpably affected by a definite marginality. These artists are marginal, however much their works may be exhibited or published. There is no doubt that there are great writers whose books appeal to readers in the hundreds of thousands. And yet nowadays a movement such as Latin American literature's boom of the 1960s and 1970s has entered an almost residual phase, in which only those whom previous decades consecrated can hold on to the mass readership that came into being then.

The portraits I offer are intended to show the way in which *variety* constitutes art's raw material. This spirit of variation switches between and superimposes very different layers such as mass culture, grand aesthetic traditions, popular cultures, the most everyday forms of language, poetic tension, private and subjective elements, and public passions. Here, exposed or hidden, are the traces of experiences that we all share. Some men and women—only a few, for whatever reason—transform these traces into material that will become an aesthetic object. Transformed into an aesthetic object, they provide a means for cognition and recognition of our *shared conditions;* they are what we are, but tauter, more precise, more focused, and also more ambiguous. Distance (aesthetic form) makes it possible to *see* more. Nobody is obliged to live the situations in which art places us. And yet, as a matter of principle, nor is anybody excluded.

Formal and semantic intensity is achieved when some men and women produce, out of what is to hand, special configurations that conform to a sort of *necessary arbitrariness.* There is no one type of artist. These portraits are aimed at encapsulating biographies in miniature, "case studies" in which each artist has her own strategies for choosing material and making decisions concerning form, for enforcing limits or transgressing them, for putting on display what she believes she knows, and for speaking or keeping quiet about what she does. There is no one way of being an artist because each individual works with tools picked up, adapted, or invented in a different way. There is no one way of being an artist because some experience and work with the signified's plenitude while others live with uncertainty as to whether anything, in the end, can be said. There is no one way of being an artist because that invisible tapestry that knits together experience and culture, reason and imagination, the known and the unknowable, is woven always with different threads.

In the name of the human race's diversity, to put this appeal in its least demanding ecological scale, we would have to conserve originals such as those seen in the following snapshots.

Snapshots

Two Optics

All his childhood he read comics and watched television. He remembers all the jingles, all the episodes of U.S. television series, and knows by heart snatches of soap opera dialog now forgotten even by their scriptwriters. He is familiar with almost all pop music and he has no prejudice concerning any hierarchy of genres, songs, or performers: He likes the best and the worst. He wanted to be a drummer, but no one in his family was prepared to put up with such an extravagance. So he bought some congas with which, at twenty years old, he toured second-rate beach cafés. While he studied painting he joined forces with the avant-garde theater and took part in the experimental staging of a Plautus play. He abandoned the theater immediately thereafter because he had no interest in taking his shoes off onstage. On television he watched all the Argentine comedies and Mexican melodramas of the 1940s and 1950s. In arthouse cinemas and special screenings he saw as much Godard as he could. He knows by heart every shot in all of Coppola's films. He skims through novels and poems; he reads newspapers and journals of the most varied sorts without skimming or skipping a line. During his only long trip to the United States he would go through the Museum of Modern Art with the same intensity that he took to the venues Tito Puente played. When friends go abroad he asks them with equal urgency to bring back books by Turner or hard-to-find salsa or Latin jazz records. He knows no barriers between cultural levels as he moves without prejudice, and often without principle, between kitsch and the sublime. He has a taste for bad taste, but without turning it into some populist demand.

He works on his drawings with the obsession of a miniaturist. While he works he talks to whoever might be nearby, he interrupts and likes to be interrupted, his distraction as intense as his concentration. He provides painstaking explanations of technical questions: on brush strokes in Chinese painting, the best paper for painting watercolors, mixing inks to obtain the subtlest range of grays set off from the darkest of blacks. His judgments about painting are briefer than his arguments about cinema. His technical training is probably more complete than his understanding of aesthetic culture. He does not look at the whole range of painting like an expert, but what he knows he knows well. When he talks of good and bad painting his judgments tend to be compact and dense, lacking any spirit of conciliation.

His drawings contain almost invisible proofs of his chaotic mixture of tastes. For years he drew diminutive figures that, seen from a "normal" distance, seem to be just symbols. These drawings have a double optic: *From afar* they are abstract compositions, in which huge vaporous masses unfold and form truncated spirals, incomplete circles, or surfaces that suggest less any geometrical pattern than the unbounded inhabitation of a canvas that at times seems to be a large fragment of an absent composition. *From afar* these drawings achieve extensive and easy movement based upon tiny symbols. Seen *close up,* these symbols reveal themselves to be diminutive figures, landscapes, castles, monsters, horses, windmills, plants straight out of science fiction, comic book heroes set in a Stone Age plot. They are saturated with cultural significations, of stories of gruesome death, icons evoking an unforeseen style of retropop, science fantasy, or fairy tales. Tolkien meets abstraction.

These drawings' dual optic can be interpreted as an aesthetic hypothesis concerning the way in which cultures mix. Their refined grays and blacks evoke a chromaticism that, as in the cinema or in comics, is resolved in black and white. What, when seen *from afar,* constitutes the drawings' abstraction reveals, when the optic is *close up,* quotations from a cultural imaginary that could not be intuited from the drawings' composition. The mix of abstraction and fictional imaginary does not result in conflict. The two optics integrate differences so that we do not see different things at the same time, but are rather able to observe two systems of representation, depending upon how our gaze is focused, each of which retains the imprints of its distinct cultural origins.

Painting and Reason

He used to speak in front of his paintings and he wouldn't let the viewer remain caught up in the ups and downs of vision. He believed that you *ought* to talk about painting, and that art (not only painting, but also the cinema, novels, music) is raw matter to be captured, encircled, interrogated, and contradicted by discourse. In front of his own work he reasoned like an intellectual. Nothing that he did suggested either the classic image of the painter given over to his or her drives as if submerged in more or less unknown waters, or even the more contemporary image of the indifferent figure unwilling to trust polemics or strong positions. Polemic was his preferred terrain: It allowed him to deploy a battery of reasons without sacrificing his taste for hyperbole. He turned dialogue into a form of aesthetic conflict rather than a means of communicating facts about the art market or about prizes.

He held on to the historic avant-garde's political tension (a type of permanent ideological alert) and interventionist style. He was invariably excessive and he knew nothing of strategies to save up aesthetic capital, to reinvest accumulated prestige, or to adopt elegant moderation in the face of gallery owners, art collectors, or critics.

He referred to his work paradoxically secure in the idea that it had nothing to say about him. It was a matter, simply and objectively, of painting. He would move from his pictures to the history of painting in a gesture that simultaneously revealed how much of the history of painting there was in his own pictures. But he was totally hostile to the postmodern penchant for collecting decorative allusions or quotations. He did not see the past as though he were an archaeologist seeking to inscribe in his own paintings the residue of idiosyncratic encounters with tradition. Like a true modern, he knew the tradition well enough to risk seeming erudite or pedantic. His decisions followed a well-reasoned path. He chose to quote only in order to show that part of the act of painting is a reflection concerning painting's methods and its past. He worked over the stars of the Russian avant-garde, the icons of Expressionism, and the still lifes of Realist representation, to whom he dedicated a virtuosity that allowed him loyally to point up Realism's limits. He painted a white fruit bowl on a white mantelpiece, as if in premonitory homage to Malevich, whom he would cite many times in his late work. Even when his pictures clearly cite other pictures of his own, they are far from introspection, repetition, or narcissism. This unabashed citing of his own work was another moment of aesthetic reflection.

His pictures inspire a delight that belongs more to the realm of the senses than to that of reason. This delight comes to us like some persistent illumination, but running through it is also the antidecorative notion of conceptual gravity. An explosion of color underlies distorted, obscure, and unsettling symbols produced by brushwork that is simultaneously free-flowing and constricted. We find a disturbing abstract syntax linking a series of pleasant, everyday objects. A simple table-cloth made of rubber becomes a hyperrealist nightmare with its fruit endlessly reiterated as though they constituted a geometrical pattern. Planes intersect the revolution's shining stars to destroy the stability offered by their five perfect points. Half a canvas is covered by the richest and most decorative of reds while the other half looks more like a skeleton penciled in with great detail to show the still unpainted picture's future. Mirrors interrogate the artificially photogenic representation of family groups because our position as spectators becomes implicated in the pattern (parents and children, kids gathered together) such that peaceful contemplation is disallowed. Chairs, brooches, and hammers float in a nonrepresentative space, in a purely plastic background.

The element of delight in his painting is a celebration that it is still possible to paint even after all that has happened in preceding decades. It is still possible to paint even after conceptual art, installations, happenings, or art as political manifesto. And yet, there was a point to what these movements achieved. He discovered it was not enough simply to show delight. So, and without denying any experimentation, the object of his painting was both the reason lying behind beauty and the beauty of reason itself.

Birds

He spends a lot of time watching birds. He has collected books on the subject and has a pair of binoculars, rubber boots, a straw hat, and a water bottle. In short, he has every-thing needed for bird-watching whether it be on a lagoon, on the plain, among reeds or in an estuary, by rivers or, of course, in woods or eucalyptus scrub. He explains that bird-watchers collect memories, because all that are left after their expedi-tions are lines written in a notebook, saying: I saw such and such a bird, male or female, on its own or with others, flying or at rest, near its nest or out looking for food, hunting earth-worms or picking at breadcrumbs, taking a dip in a pond or perched on a branch. Then the sighting's precise time and lo-cation are noted. Additionally there is a note as to whether the sighting is rare, common, or exceptional (along a scale to be found in bird-watching books). Incidentally, looking at birds made his eyes sharper to notice nature's comings and goings and the landscape's variations. He knows how reflections in water look at midday compared to later in the afternoon, the differences between clouds, the effect of a few reeds on a little girl's face or on a jetty's wooden boards. This, at the same time, sharpened his attention for variations of whatever type. At times the differences between birds are so small that you have to concentrate upon details. And light is simply either di-rect sunlight or shade only for those who have not spent hours watching the light changing imperceptibly but inexorably as it passes over a branch or a meadow.

He has always been interested in variations. He reads an-notated editions of books that contain all the variants a text went through as its author wrote and revised. Also he collects bilingual editions in order to trace in cabalistic detail all the slippages that take place when words pass from one language to another. His taste for variation led him to learn Latin, be-cause there is nothing that changes so exaggeratedly as a lan-guage no longer spoken. In the different versions of Latin you can read each of the different translators' culture and history. Little by little he, too, put his hand to translation. He enjoys word games: He uses a dictionary that lets him look up Span-ish words as if they were English and so put together poems that are absurd yet perfectly resonant as poetry.

There is an intimate link between these tastes and his own

literature. He has often written the names of birds into poems whose landscape is delicate and peaceful. A glimpse of reflected light or the sound of water are the briefest of revelations of landscape, for which you have to lie in wait ready to write them down before they disappear. They can then be taken up an infinite number of times, but they always keep their quality of having captured a snatch of time in the blink of an eye. The poems he writes like this are intensely objective and clearly personal at the same time. They retain something of a mode of experiencing the world that is visual rather than dramatic or psychological. His writing deals with the plenitude of sensations in the world, even when he knows that each of these words raises a philosophical problem: plenitude, sensations, world?

He elaborates variations upon the text itself: versions in which, at times, what changes is the rhythm; at other times, a few words; at others, a verb tense; or one that introduces, for the attentive ear, delicate changes in the way it sounds; finally, in other versions everything changes. He is perfectly able to explain why he has corrected what he has corrected. Just as he reads other poets with great care, so he knows how to read his own writing with equal care.

When he corrects something in one version without discarding the previous version, his readers are able to see the poem as clearly as though he were composing it inside a crystal box.

Conversation

He likes the simple jokes he learned in the final years of primary school and laughs, splitting his sides, at the crudest of word games. For him, the art of conversation is not an exercise in competence or an extension of his literature into daily life, but rather a proof of friendship that has to be affectionate, bantering, and welcoming even though, on occasion, it may end in fights of Homeric proportions. His conversation is made up of feints, of familiar tidbits, from which come fragments of sentences, or anecdotes told so clumsily that you would think he hardly knew how to relate an event or depict a character. His irony is always too forceful and the joke all too often ruins any effect that does not depend completely upon what is taken as read or unsaid. He delights in pointing out what is completely obvious and he hardly ever strives for originality in his observations. He does not care about seeming intelligent.

And yet throughout these long, threadbare conversations, his eyes, by contrast, are searching and alive, as though his sense of sight were looking for what his words do not even care to communicate. There is someone, within, lying in wait; sometimes he pounces, for example when he delivers a political diatribe, when he makes the harshest of moral judgments, or when, eventually, he is provoked by the mention of a writer whom he loves or despises.

He is a man from the provinces who lives in Paris with the cold and unamused distance of someone who is ill-disposed to buy any of the trinkets on offer in the cultural market. Not even when it concerns his own work is he disposed to participate in such lowly transactions. He refuses to play any part in what he sees as the nightmarish way in which literature is treated on television. He wants people to read him, but is incapable of seeking praise in a way that would cultivate a literary career and demand of him a dedication that he reserves for literature alone.

His choice of reading is idiosyncratic and follows a system that is difficult to comprehend fully in that at times his declared reading seems doubtful while at other times he feigns not to have read authors who are surely influences on him. In any case, it is known that he admires Adorno, Sartre, Borges, Juan L. Ortiz, César Vallejo, and Antonioni. It is also common knowledge that from the outset he has harbored an irritated and intolerant critical attitude toward what has been called the Latin American new novel or the Latin American literary boom. Gabriel García Márquez figures among his favorite targets, of course. He never believed that Manuel Puig was a great writer.

His fictional work is both compact and extensive. Here

also he does not care about seeming intelligent. The only perfection he seeks takes poetry as the be-all and end-all. And yet
his characters and plots prove to be unexpectedly interesting
if you take into account that they are almost always the same,
outlined in identical landscapes, and concerned with arguments over what are really trivialities. His literature is difficult, especially if you hope to find ideas and arguments that
can be quoted and summarized. It has to be read like poetry,
very slowly, so you grasp in the sentence rhythm and the raw
matter of the words themselves the very gradual advance of
stories that are literally *stuck to language*. He, too, could reg-
ister his aesthetic program as being "behind you is beloved
language."

Time drags in his novels, as if it would never pass, though
soon enough it is clear that it has passed forever. His descriptions seem to point to something that can be grasped, but,
later, they are repeated and the landscape changes so much
that description becomes no more than a wager against the
world's multiplicity encircled but never completely captured
by literature. The drama of the human condition arises not
from any especially dramatic incidents, but rather from the
presence of what remains unknown to us, from the presence of
what, probably, will never be revealed in all its truth. And yet
the question of truth retains meaning even however much he
may have learned that an answer is unlikely. He knows that
meaning is difficult but that to renounce meaning is a banality.

His writing is a perfect demonstration of just how far writing can go.

Irony

He has been writing from a very young age. The first thing of
his I read, over ten years ago, was a few pages imitating the
style of a writer he admires even today. But what distinguished
the imitation from its model was its depiction, written with a
certain violence, of an event that the admired writer would
probably not have chosen: It dealt with the concentrated and
laborious progress of a dog shitting. At around the same time,

he wrote a long article about this same admired writer, in the course of which he had the misfortune to enrage his subject. The young writer remained undaunted. Since then, he has published a number of novels.

He studied literature at the university while working as a taxi driver. He was given, and almost immediately resigned, a post in the university. He also abandoned the taxi without going on to wear himself out looking for jobs that would necessarily be tied in to literature. He took a quiet interest in literary theory; in any case, it remains clear that the only thing that really interests him is literature itself. He holds on to some loyal friendships from the literary world, but never took up the practice of hanging around writers as though it were a duty writers undertook to make sure they were recognized among their peers. His peers respect him, although perhaps they think he is a little reserved.

His relation to language surprises you as much when you listen to him as when you read him. His parents were immigrants, and he is a Jew by birth; in conversation he resorts to a demotic form of River Plate Spanish full of words and turns of phrase that are no longer in use. He does not explain where he has taken them from. But is it not this trait of picturesque originality that distinguishes him from others? His most personal trademark is irony. For the majority of people, irony is one form through which to consider and present their thoughts, a form that may be used often or sparingly, but which does not become their sole discursive mode. By contrast, in his case irony is a permanent trait that he never completely abandons. It may lie on the surface in the phrases he employs, or it may be found in a slight alteration of tone; it may play openly with conflicting meanings or may be disguised through very light touches. Whatever the case, it is always there.

It is therefore very difficult to be at all sure that you understand what he is saying. His interlocutors are permanently suspended in a state of indecision, not so much over any given meaning in particular, but rather more generally over the meaning of everything said. Is he congratulating someone or making fun of them? When he affirms something, is it for real or quite the reverse? To date his literature has deployed this ironic destiny in a number of different ways, principally in a use of words that twists and bends their meanings. But this is not a case of overobvious twists that would make a point of contradicting language's usual meanings.

On the contrary, it is a case of infinitesimally small deviations from common meanings, opening up cracks in words' surfaces that do not become impossible obstacles but rather brief moments of hesitation. When we read his novels our situation is one of continuous but attenuated insecurity. At times words hardly seem to correspond at all to their customary meaning, and at times they twist or deviate such that they are turned around and become "incorrect," or they seek to expand their sphere of meaning such that they take over the place of other words.

He writes as though he looked at language out of the corner of his eye, not out of distrust (which would be almost commonplace) but as though he had no recollection of language, as though it were both some instrument he understands perfectly and yet at the same time also a strange new land that has still to be fully possessed. It would be wrong to think that his relationship with language is insecure; it's a case rather of a transversal perspective across a space that we habitually look at full on. Through his writing he explores trails that head off to one side and paths that deviate from the main track.

Sleepless

She woke up in the silence of the small hours. Her husband slept in a space set off nearby. The house rustled with almost imperceptible eddies of sound. She moved some papers around. Nothing. She could only think of the house's other, sleeping, inhabitant. He was the great writer, a man who held his passions back and made them public at the same time, the poet touched by the gods and by fame. Her admiration for him was as powerful as her desire to outdo him.

What brought them together to the point of tearing them

apart, that night and over the days that followed, was an attack on words carried out almost blindly, an attempt to swim against the current through a fluid simultaneously resistant and insubstantial. What brought them together was a common good, though the more fortunate of the two would keep leaving his own distinct footprint along the way. What brought them together was also the pursuit of favor, the hope of triumph as they went about their business presenting their own work, and the idea that they had a mission that should be recognized by others (who had no mission to accomplish). What brought them together was the difference between them and the more radical difference that separated them from other men and women. What brought them together was a love of beauty, which they held up as a superior passion, and of fame, which they considered to be part of an exchange in which they gave more than they received. What brought them together, without doubt, was respect for the tools of their trade, and the conviction that there was only a certain point to which one could learn to use them, combined with the belief that the work they were carrying out could sap their energy beyond all limit. They were engaged in a search.

Fully awake now but unable to write a single line, but lacking any desire to read or watch or listen to anything, she thought that he would sleep in peace unaware that, right then, she was thinking about him with an admiration chilled by envy or, better, with a residual envy that admiration would make superfluous. At any rate youth was on her side. She compared what the two of them had written and the age at which they published their first books. There were still some years to go before the woman who could not sleep would reach the age at which the man sleeping way over there had achieved his first great triumph or, if you like, his first great work of art. There was no doubt that admiration for an old man perturbed her less than admiration for a contemporary. But the old man had to stay alive, because his death would end any possibility that he would recognize, at last, that she was his equal. Despite everything, more brought them together than drove them apart. Would that not include the religion that was art, the republic of letters, or the shared attempt to pursue beauty and truth? Would it not include the fact that they worked on the same raw materials with the same tools, that they read hundreds of books, or that they felt an irrecuperable distance from the repeated ups and downs of everyday life? Perhaps it was the idea that they competed in the same social space and that their competition did not so much differentiate the two of them as it differentiated them both from the rest of the human race, the obsession with failure and with success, or the fact that they wavered between believing that they had triumphed and believing they had failed.

What, finally, did bring them together? Did they worship at the same church, were they members of the same party, or did they like the same wines and the same landscapes? Possibly they would not even be moved by the same books or would not cite the same lines from a poet they had both read. And yet the woman realized that the importance of discovering what brought them together was that it might erase the distance that kept them apart. But in the end, what was there to discover? Perhaps they would find the truth of envy, the source of an intense friendship with a man she hardly knew, the sense of wonder before a work of art judged worthy of admiration, the forward march toward a place where perhaps neither of them would find what they were looking for, where they would find only tiredness and vanity, or perhaps the imagination that enabled writing alongside the imagination that suffocated writing. "You feel your way forward blindly, even while you know almost all that there is to be known." "That," the man who was surely asleep said once to the woman now awake, "that is art."

How could one make such a grand claim? "Secure in the knowledge that others have no option but to recognize that it is our right," he replied almost without stopping to think. Such are the rules of the game on which these two are set with an intensity that makes one think in terms of excess, though it may also wear the mask of indifferent distance. Others recognize that it is their right. They are permitted to center themselves upon that right, to use it, to make it produce (if possible) the greatest book of all time. But who can say calmly "the greatest book of all time" as though knowing what that meant? Still wide awake, the woman thought that that was another question altogether. And there she might perhaps be right.

Values and the Market

For centuries a handful of men and a few exceptional women took part in a long and intractable conversation about art. There was a little of everything: disputes between poets; quarrels between those on the side of the classics on the one hand and innovators who argued for the virtues of the moderns on the other; the occasional physical scuffle in theater boxes; and young film directors prepared to respond to audience whistles by throwing stones. There were lifelong rivalries and loyalties, persecutions, suicides, works of art destroyed both by their owners and by others, sublime sacrifices, and vile deceits. The name of art was invoked in each of these skirmishes, even if their protagonists could not always show that they were moved solely by what all considered to be this noblest of causes. In any case, the argument went on in its various incarnations. There was a time when authority was understood to reside in figures external to the field of art itself. These authorities made plans over artists' heads, and acted like princes or priests, defining the meaning and point of view of what was produced. Later these authorities let the world of art be free to determine its own direction, and artists thought that they were the ones to be, precisely, the sole princes and priests in their own republic. Later still, other artists, who had started out at society's margins, arrived on the scene to say that neither external authorities nor established artists but rather bohemians, "angry women," missionaries, or, finally, the producers who put their products on the market should legislate for art.

Until a few decades ago, anyone taking part in any of these controversies did so thinking that the positions they took were based in fundamental values whose superiority could be demonstrated rationally or through an appeal to forms of reason beyond aesthetic reason. This kingdom may have been crisscrossed by struggles between opposing programs or personalities, but it was in itself stable and sovereign. You knew (or you thought you knew, which is effectively the same thing) why what you were defending was better than what you were attacking. The argument's interest or importance was never in doubt, because it laid out fundamental differences concerning art's enjoyment as much as its production.

Almost every word I have just written is now subject to dispute. I hear it said that the argument is unproductive, that its terms are mistaken, or that it conceals its true motivations. I hear it said that you can no longer pose questions about the nature of art. The question holds no interest for a certain cultivated indifference that goes under the heading of postmodernism. Meanwhile the sociology of culture responds from a perspective concerned only with institutions: It would say that art is whatever a specific specialized group of people collectively decide it should be. Can this response be incorporated into a discussion of aesthetics? Is there any escape from a definition of art that refers only to institutions?

They assure us that it is only possible to talk about the nature of art by enumerating, first, the functions art performs in the life of a society. Then, they tell us, we need to make an inventory of the various beliefs about art held by artists, critics, publishers, and even the Sunday supplements (which would not be granted such responsibility in other areas of social judgment). They tell us that art is what it is and that it is what it is because social conventions agree that that is what it should be. Set against the essentialist fervor that once searched for art's fundamentals we find a perspective borrowed from the sociology of culture. This sociology of culture has worked away like acid at essentialism, elitism, and the mysticism of differentiation (all of which would make up the sickness that affects aesthetic sovereignty) by piecing together the elements of institutional constructions in a way that seems convincing if you judge by its capacity to describe art's social functions.

In short, to consider art as an institution implies locating it somewhere *irreverently down to earth* where the apparent arbitrariness of exceptionality is dissolved given that social movements, drives, and regulations are also seen to be acting in the sphere of art. A perspective predicated upon institutions lays bare the fantasies that artists weave around their practice and reveals that they are ruled by economic and social determinants as much as are those who spend their time producing commodities or competing for power. There is but one particularity: All this happens only through the mediation of forces and forms that belong to the specific field within which artists are active.

In modernity the relations between artists and audience, writers and publishers, painters and dealers, or even among cultural producers themselves, operate within a *space articulated as a field of competing forces*. These forces are not a direct reflection of the tendencies that confront each other in other areas of society; rather they make up a structure specific to the world of art itself. Within this structure, artists take up positions depending on the cultural patrimony that they have inherited or accumulated for themselves. Position-takings within the intellectual field cannot escape the forces that really control them, including the search to consecrate and legitimate the artists' own production, and the competition between artists expressed in their strategic struggles and alliances. This is no sacred field of art, but is rather *a profane space of conflict*. Alert sociologists (Pierre Bourdieu is exemplary) study discourses to discover what they deny or conceal. The discourse of artistic disinterest reveals its truth only if it is seen as a form of long-term economic investment. Artists *take up positions in order to position their work* and by doing so they remain blind to the truth of their own practice. When they speak of art, they are also speaking about competition; even when they seem most obsessed with the search for artistic form, they always have an eye out for the market and for their potential audience.

This sociology of culture is a reduction of aesthetic positions that brings them back down to relations of force within the intellectual field. The reading it proposes, taking up precisely the "rules of art" as they are discussed by writers and artists among themselves, fails to consider a number of questions. When every declaration taking a stand within an aesthetic dispute is interpreted simply as a search for legitimacy or prestige, what then happens to conflict? When freedom is but one ideology among many, to which we subscribe only to disguise our less ethereal desires for consecration, what then happens to the ability to choose? When we are assured that they are but betting chips thrown on the table at which what is at stake is always the monopoly of cultural legitimacy, what then happens to aesthetic values?

Artists' actions may well be driven by the rules of this game. But while the sociology of culture manages to dislodge idiotic notions of disinterest and aesthetic priesthood, it equally soon dispenses with any analysis of those properly aesthetic resistances that produce art's semantic and formal density. As well as doing away with the myths of absolutely free creativity, it also does away with the problem of value.

Sociological perspectives make any clear conscience achieved through self-justification evaporate, but they also eat away at the density of purposes that lie behind art. From such a perspective, Marcel Duchamp's gesture of choosing a urinal as a work of art suitable for gallery exhibition loses any element of surprise. Quite the opposite, Duchamp would merely have been ahead of his time in providing a limit case for the theory of art as institution, and his urinal-work is that theory's capstone. The object was *made* through the artist's own aesthetic vision, there being nothing in the object itself that could be considered to have any intrinsic aesthetic value; indeed, the urinal is an attempt to do away with such values permanently. We have reached the limit of art as a set of conventions when value adheres solely to the gesture performed in the artist's choice of object, the work itself having no other foundation than institutional relations. These relations made it possible for Duchamp to choose the urinal and for this choice to be accepted by those in the know.

What in the early years of this century could be seen as a decisive moment for the avant-gardes can now also be read as the final chapter in art's desacralization. Duchamp's gesture furnishes the sociological gaze with "crucial experience." It further sets off a conflagration that will also consume the avant-gardes, that is, the best that twentieth-century art has produced.

With the avant-garde, art reaches a limit familiar also elsewhere in twentieth-century society. If anything goes, then the core or spinal column of what was once art's domain now disappears. The task proper to art was once precisely the struggle to define problems differently from how they had been defined in the past and from how others were defining them in the present, and to come up with new solutions. Now, however, on the one hand the sociology of culture teaches that aesthetic movements should be read as battles for legitimacy and consecration. On the other hand, with the intervention of the avant-gardes (for the sociology of art, paradigmatic of art in general), any possibility of considering values independent of those instituted by the artist's gaze simply evaporates. Moreover, any analysis is deferred still further as the legitimation of the artist's gaze, in turn, depends upon other gazes, belonging to other artists, the gallery owner who accepts their work, or the publisher publishing it.

Caught in this double bind, the traditional debate over aesthetics has lost its foundation, probably forever. There is now no god, extrinsic or intrinsic to the space of art, to impart the sacred book that would lay out the values to be found in art. The desacralization process has reached its conclusion. One of its merits is to have instituted aesthetic relativism, also one of its most worrying consequences. Relativism is like democracy: Once people hear what it claims to offer, all else crumbles before the leveling and egalitarian impulse that drives it. But whereas we might view optimistically the idea of some form of "constitutional agreement" over what should be done in the political sphere, it is hard to see how it can be adequate to the problems of value and taste in art. In art, more than in any other sphere, establishing the bounds of the possible is as difficult as delineating what should be forbidden. This difficulty frustrates censorship, whose arguments (whether religious, political, national, or revolutionary) can be backed only by force. When democracy takes over the sphere of art, it also institutes pluralism as the principle by which to regulate differences between distinct positions. This pluralism ensures the postulate of universal equivalence that could be expressed as the idea that "all styles seem more or less equivalent and equally (un)important." Nobody can be condemned for their ideas about aesthetics, but then nor will anybody have the tools allowing them to compare, discuss, or confirm aesthetic differences. The market, well versed in abstract equivalents, welcomes this aesthetic pluralism as the ideology that most suits its needs.

And yet there is still an interrupted conversation to be continued. For centuries a handful of men and a few exceptional women argued about art *as if* discussing the values it brings were possible. This "fiction" provided the frame for art's dynamism and at the same time, at least in the West, the impulse for its productivity. Equally, the hypothesis that there exist values whose foundation could be located within the aesthetic sphere instigated the processes by which the aesthetic sought independence from religion, politics, traditional authorities, and from power. Nowadays the idea of this independence is a commonplace even in those situations where censorship prevents it from being exercised. But other problems arise within this commonplace. If those in power can have no more secure basis for their opinion than artists, then artists' opinions, conversely, gain what force they have only insofar as they can gain resources from one of two other places, the field of art itself or the market.

Sociology believes it can demonstrate that the values attacked or defended within the field of art are generated by a logic that is specific to art only in that it regulates the relations between artists, not insofar as it is a logic concerned with art itself. If this is the case, there is then another stage on which a truth about aesthetic values unfolds. Moreover, the basis of these values should then be found more in the laws of competition between artists than in the "rules of art." The effect of the movement of permanent change, the religion of "the new" and the search for "originality" (modern art's slogans) was to melt away established aesthetic authorities. This process weakened the weight of tradition and permitted an endless series of confrontations to unfold between those defending strongholds established within the artistic field and those arriving from outside it to take these strongholds over. In this war of position, the young—artists who did not cultivate links with the elites, or intellectuals who could locate their origins in the people—argued for their own rights through recourse to aesthetic differentiations and also to slogans taken from outside the discourse of aesthetics. But the flip side of this story is that competition indicated the truth of what was denied by those who took part in such rivalry. Aesthetic difference was not simply a matter of aesthetics and at its limit could well be considered something else altogether: a misrecognized struggle for ascendance.

If we accept this description, then a claim to "disinterest" in the discussion of aesthetic values is simply yet another ideology working to unify the republic of artists by guaranteeing them an identity upheld by imaginary virtues (such as the love of art, the representation of those who have no voice, the defense of tradition or the discovery of the new, the construction of nationhood, or the search for beauty or justice). Ideas of a mission in the world, of prophetic tension, of a retreat to art as the one place where concessions mean nothing, or, on the contrary, the idea of jumping into society in order to fulfil one's destiny there—all these would be fictions whose true motives, as in a detective story, would have to be found in the shadows. With no basis in established authorities, and with no self-sufficient basis in the terrain of art, the objectivity of aesthetic values has been given up as a dead duck.

This tough law also applies to the critics, however much they once believed they could speak about art from the point of view of a knowledge that let them see something different from what artists saw and something more than what the public or the audience saw. Their judgment is now seen to have as much or as little basis as that of artists themselves. Thus there would seem to be no other way out of this quandary than to adopt relativism in all its tolerance, though this is a position that would have precluded the avant-gardes of the twentieth century as surely as it would have meant that the art of the nineteenth century, from Romanticism to Impressionism, would likewise have been unimaginable. These movements felt themselves called toward the absolute, and their aesthetic experimentation was unabashedly undertaken in the name of convictions that were exclusionary, partisan, and antagonistic. Each position that triumphed also bears legible traces of alternatives rejected, which may have been repressed as illegitimate or abandoned as old-fashioned.

I am putting things this way because I am interested in taking sociological description and its consequences *absolutely literally*. What we habitually call postmodernity (by which we might mean a "condition" leavened with the crisis of the historical avant-gardes mixed with the residue of paradigms that might guarantee a minimum of objectivity) had its prophets, for whom we would have to look precisely among the voices that exposed the blind confidence the moderns placed in their rationality. And I am not referring simply to postmodernity's philosophical genealogy, but also to the corrosion produced by sociological and anthropological approaches that, less imaginatively but stubbornly and persistently, showed us the hollowness of modernity's foundations and, consequently, the vanity of any attempt to construct limits and legislate over art. In this sense, the postmodern condition's inspiration is inevitably sociological. *Sociology provides postmodernity's self-*

understanding, allowing it to install value relativism as its ʌ, ochal horizon.

Postmodernism has dislodged the fiction that once enabled modernity's doubleheadedness. This consisted of its universalist calling and its tendency to do away with difference on the one hand; and on the other, its desire for objectivity and rationality that stand in sharp relief to an immense unfolding of subjectivity, individuality, and emphatic marks of differentiating style. As fissures opened up in this spirit we call modern, those who, aware of history's twists and turns, tried to devise a way forward found themselves losing support for this project; today all that seems possible is to acknowledge that there is a multiplicity of possible paths. In the West at least, artists' and intellectuals' vocation toward the absolute is now perhaps permanently weakened; there is one institution, however, unfolding as the new paradigm for multiple liberties. This is the market. Specifically what concerns us here is the market of symbolic goods.

I want to gauge the consequences of the changes I have just described. The existence and recognition of, and dispute over, sites of special authority regarding aesthetic material entailed artists raising their voices to challenge "common sense" judgment and brandishing their credentials to support the proselytizing diffusion of their opinions. Unwelcome though it may be, the fact is that the principles and values affecting aesthetic (or, when it comes to it, philosophical) material were not connected in any direct manner to the number of followers garnered by any particular object or text. As has often been said, knowledge delimited a sacred zone providing the basis for new sources of power distinct from those instituted by religious revelation or tradition.

One of modernity's paradoxes is, precisely, this relation between knowledge and power, which are fused in a more tangled manner than simple descriptions would seem to show. Regarding forms of knowledge (among them the "rules of art"), modernity could be liberal without being democratic;

indeed, at times it could be absolutely illiberal. Hence a certain distrust toward "common sense" runs through the history of conceptions of art and culture. As a result, when modernity takes notice of democratic pressures, it turns to pedagogy and the idea that the majority need to have their taste educated, on the assumption that there is no cultural spontaneity that would ensure good judgment on aesthetic questions. The same motivation could be said to lie behind the most diverse variants of political pedagogy.

Modernity combined this pedagogic ideal with an unfolding of the market of symbolic goods beyond any hitherto conceivable limit. But in this double movement modernity would come across an unforeseen lesson. The market and what would come to be called the "culture industry" undermined the bases for authority that had once made it appropriate to think in terms of a pedagogical paradigm for aesthetic material. There were some who perceived this contradiction very early on; their diagnosis was that "industrial art" meant a death sentence for those refined values that the cultural elites saw as their own and wanted spread propagandistically or defended at the last ditch, depending on the case. The market inevitably introduces quantitative evaluative criteria that frequently contradict critics' aesthetic arbitrations or artists' opinions. The very idea of popularity could not but be looked upon with mistrust given that it provides the basis for the contradiction that lies at the heart of democracy. Over the past two hundred years there have been those who predicted catastrophic results should the opinion of the majority be let loose in matters of art and culture; others replied that they preferred to run the risks of democratizing fine arts and letters, trusting in the effectiveness of pedagogic institutions (whose power, however, also slowly began to crumble). These two issues, audience expansion and the decline of values, were locked in mortal combat. Yet so long as the pedagogic paradigm could be sustained, the conflict did not take on all the characteristics of an irresolvable dilemma.

Should we accept that this combat has indeed been mortal

and try to get out of the dilemma by what seems to be the only half-open door? I am referring to the emergency exit discovered by the cultural neopopulism that finds in market symptoms a capitalist replacement for the old romantic notion of the People. Taking this emergency exit leads to some nasty surprises unless you choose to close your eyes to a few important questions. The first of these is the iron law of the market, profit. It is no good simply to declare some old-fashioned condemnation of profit, as this would only serve to ease intellectuals' sense of morality. But one would hope that tolerance would not be bound up so amicably with a failure to see what is going on. It is not fashionable to talk of the market of symbolic goods in terms of profit, the maximization of earnings, or economic competition; yet no one would think of putting aside these terms when dealing with any other market. The sociology of culture has pointed out ways in which artists operate in a manner that prevents us from considering the aesthetic field as a kingdom of free spirits whose only motivation comes from art itself. However limited this description may be, it is, I believe, less restrictive than the narrow-minded market optimism that celebrates the replacement of aesthetic authority by an atomized agglomeration of consumers.

If the market triumphs, what then is the future of that art that is not and perhaps never will be mass art, or of that art that does not play the game of becoming merchandise to tickle the fancy of the capitalist actors who define the way the market goes? Some answers to this question can be found in what we nowadays call the cultural policies developed by States that do not trust the mercantile dynamic to take care of culture's destiny as a whole.

But this is not the perspective that I am interested in developing here. I hope rather to return to a question about the institution of taste and values. Let us recapitulate certain presuppositions: Let us grant that the old certainties elaborated by artists and philosophers are now in crisis because any aesthetic legitimation when examined up close comes down to a struggle for social legitimation; that the problematic of the relation between aesthetic representation and society, the dynamic of the new, and the very project of the avant-gardes have all been explained by the laws that govern competition between artists and that regulate struggles to impose institutional definitions of art; that value relativism can be considered the only strong belief passed down from modernity to postmodernity. If all this is so, the question now arises: Is there any site, other than the market, in which the institution of values is imaginable? The market amplifies other voices that have no authority to speak within artist society. In the market, the public or audience, whose form of knowledge is unspecific, has as much weight as those who have specific knowledges. In the last instance it is the viewing public who will decide whether critical opinions or artists' declarations seem pertinent, helpful, welcome, acceptable, or entertaining. The public will grant to some individuals the always temporary possibility of indicating the way in which taste is moving. The public will likewise be able to revoke this concession without having to explain the reasons for such a fall into disgrace. It will crown one artist and dethrone another who was in favor only the day before. A given audience will have the power to undervalue or ignore, to celebrate or respect, and to ensure its preferences are heard to the extent allowed by the weight of its interventions in the market, all of which are transformed by some alchemy and through diverse mechanisms (the best-seller list or the ticket office) into public opinion. Specialist authority will never fully recover. Experts once brought knowledge and power together by articulating what was modernity's convincing and critical vision; the unlimited expansion of the market means that they now have to look elswhere for the power once granted them by their comrades in arms and the public alike.

There are today multiple sources of legitimacy. It is not enough to speak out on the basis that some small group of people has granted you that right. Unless you want to speak for that small group alone, you will have to gain some other authority that does not depend totally on discourse, let alone on those who are experts on discourse, nor even on some theoretical "everyone." It is true that the community of artists and critics still hands out praise, building reputations and organizing hierarchies. But this building and organizing takes place only where it is still powerful, which may be because it has been granted power, because it has not completely lost power, because the market needs to legitimate itself through its authority, because the State has decided to deal with it in line with specific policies, or because the art lobby has kept hold of communication channels to other lobbies. The face-off between market and artists has reached different resolutions in different parts of the West. Moreover, the forces sitting around a negotiating table do not have the same capacity for action or equal means of intervening in the market and thus passing democracy's test of success.

The problem is quite complicated, which is not to say that it has arrived out of the blue. What we face now is the result of a long leveling process. The crisis of objectivity, the disappearance of "proof," anxiety over foundations, and the way in which beliefs legitimating the status quo have been dissolved only to be replaced by new, antihierarchical beliefs are all chapters of a history whose results in the political field include the republican reliance on institutions, a certain form of populism, and democracy as a political ideology. Along the way, some forms of knowledge became separated from power, circulated through society, and became allied with those who had been divested of prestigious forms of knowledge, to confront traditional forms of knowledge and established positions of power. The opinion of the common person became an inextricable dimension of public opinion.

The democratic revolution introduced its dilemmas and paradoxes into the field of art almost two hundred years ago. But we had to wait until midway through the twentieth century for this antihierarchical leveling process to combine with the culture industry and especially with the mighty mass communications media. Today, however, this combination seems indissoluble. With the passing of time, the audience has not only expanded, but also has gained autonomy from more traditional institutions, which were controlled by experts who saw their role in terms of educating taste. Instead, the public audience has started an unending dialogue with other experts, those we today call mass media intellectuals. Audience growth and antihierarchical tendencies are simply two sides of the same coin. They are phenomena that appear at the same time, and we cannot expect the miracle of keeping hold of the one without slipping into the other.

But we are not forced to believe that all the effects of this expansive, leveling process should be celebrated with one voice. We have special reason to doubt if the market, surely an essential space of circulation and distribution, also adds to its egalitarian tendencies an antiegalitarianism based upon the concentration of economic power. We are not forced to celebrate the decline of artists' and intellectuals' authority when it comes about through the ascent of those who manage the culture industry. I should hardly need to say this: *The cultural market does not set the stage for a community of free consumers and producers.*

If relativism is an ideal of toleration, then the market of symbolic goods is not the space in which this ideal can develop fully. It would be better to say that the market acts something like a consulate for taste. Some products can move around with preferential, multiple-entry visas; others are favored with protectionist, diplomatic visas; a few are deported; while a considerable number have serious problems gaining entry clearance. Taste is formed through the collision and alliance of all these tendencies. In the name of value relativism, and in lieu of other criteria of differentiation—precisely because value's foundations have been eaten away—everything operates *as if* the market were the ideal space of pluralism. I say "as if" because you could argue that the market governs through forceful interventions affecting both artists and audience more than through value neutrality. *Market absolutism* replaces old forms of authority, especially when it comes to those artistic productions that are linked to the media industry.

Market neopopulists and those who defend value relativism in art alike both end up, if by different routes, undermining the basis of aesthetics, itself already exposed by the so-

ciological perspective's profane mechanicism. Art's desacralization appears to follow inevitably from these two broad movements, both of which were absolutely part of the script laid
out by modernity's logic. In general it is hard to lament the retreat of authorities that were based in exclusion or traditional-
ism. Still, there is some indication that the charisma that once
belonged to the artist, as the mark of his or her exceptional
condition, survives. It is just that charisma has just now been
transferred to other agents, and we are yet to see whether or
not they will go down in history bathed in the same ennobling
aura that now makes them stand out. In any case, those consecrated by the market alone are as unwilling as the cultural heroes that preceded them to adopt a relativistic perspective. We
might pay more regard to these pretensions were they not accompanied by the exercise of a new form of absolutism; and
this new absolutism rests upon notions that deserve as close an
examination as did the formerly dominant ideas that were
shattered some decades ago. The market of symbolic goods is
not neutral and it shapes tastes just like any other institution
that might have preceded it, setting up evaluative criteria, turning on accumulated cultural capital, and colonizing even that
terrain that was opened up by this century's avant-gardes.
When it comes to mass audiences, the market, along with
some institutions linked directly or indirectly to its laws of
motion, has a similar authority to the traditional charismatic
prestige or the modes of consecration specific to the modernity
that it replaces.

The market has some very interesting things to say about
art: about how an aesthetic is imposed upon the North American West Coast; about how an artist's stock rises if she has her
work shown in a retrospective exhibition at the Pompidou;
about how much a couple of reviews in the *New York Times* or
three reports in a Latin American paper are worth in building
fame; or about how much more weight an Oscar has compared
to a prize at Cannes, or vice versa. What the market has to say
is hardly insignificant: It forms part of a map whose landmarks
depend upon both customs and institutions. Culture's public

audience moves around this changing cartography, at times picking out one part of the terrain or another, at other times herded to those zones that suit the market. Some sectors of this viewing public always occupy the same strips of land, as if they were fenced in; others have learned to spread out among different regions and to choose their own destinations. But no one has limitless freedom in their movements, and the poorest of all, those who are least privileged, are prisoners of their place of origin.

Evaluative neutrality suggests that the most democratic way is to think that everything is possible and equally legitimate. The history of art would be a huge warehouse to which anyone could resort without there being any rules to govern the entry or exit of merchandise. Yet the way things are does not allow such optimism. What has come about is a rift between artists and the mass audience—a rift that the avant-gardes once cultivated as their sign of difference, but that at the same time they wanted to exorcize by breaking art's institutionally set limits. In the context of this rift, the market works for its own ends rather than for some utopia of aesthetic egalitarianism. And this rift offers little of interest for a discussion of art. The absolutism that aesthetic relativism installs is another of modernity's paradoxes, perhaps its final one. Here too the other face of a position of triumph, however justified, turns out to be an act of barbarism.

With aesthetic value's foundations undermined, experts (whether market, academic, or media experts) are left stronger than ever. Whereas once legitimacy was won only after long struggles within the field of art, today it can be acquired from within institutions that are ever more remote from aesthetic perspectives. Even though the public's sovereignty is affirmed, there is a stubborn silence over where we believe lies the boundary marking the limits of this sovereignty's exercise. The argument over value in art excluded millions of people because, in effect, it was an argument only among those who were also actors within the field of art. The fact that today this argument has been struck off the agenda—that it is variously considered old-fashioned or imputed to follow an absolutist calling typical of the modernity we all wish to leave behind—can be seen as a sign of our times' democracy. Even if this is the case, it would still also have to be considered the result of the capitalist market's hitherto unprecedented expansion within the artistic sphere. And we know that the market, like the mythical figure of justice, is blind in the face of justice.

On the other hand, pluralism and evaluative neutrality do not mean the same thing within the sphere of art as they do from the perspective in which the differences between people or customs are to be judged. Further still, it could be said that art thrives not on the coexistence of differences but rather on the utopia of an absolute. The State and the public institutions are equanimity's guardians. Likewise, artists seem to have been more suited to exclusive positions. Perhaps it is the case that if the aesthetic sphere takes on board religious or political pluralism it means not so much the introduction of a truly revelatory sociological light as the eclipse of some of the traits that truly define the sphere.

The fact that values may be relative when compared across societies or historical periods does not make the debate about what our own values are of any less interest. Knowing that these values should not be imposed upon other cultures is a guard against absolutism; but the relativistic moral of this knowledge should not impose upon us some kind of absolutism born of defeat. When it comes to art, a strong stand that might make the argument over value possible once more could bring the aesthetic act's dense signification (the densest of contemporary society's significations) out into the open for many people. It would be worth making this stand even if we recognize that it is an illusion to hope to institute values for all eternity.

Chapter 5

Intellectuals

They thought that they were in the vanguard of society, and that they were the voice of the voiceless. They believed they could represent those who lived under the burden of poverty and ignorance, but without understanding these people's true interests or the right way to reach out to them. They thought that ideas could trickle down to the workers, peasants, or the socially marginalized, who were immersed in a world without light, prisoners to experience. They felt that they had a promise to fulfill—to secure the rights of those who had been deprived of any rights at all. They thought that they knew more than did the common people, and that this gave them but one privilege, that of communicating this knowledge and, let us be precise, imposing it upon a majority whose social condition prevented them from seeing clearly and, as a result, from acting in accord with their interests.

In societies where knowledge was becoming more and more important for the production and reproduction of life itself, they discovered that the forms of knowledge to which they had access were also a source of power. At times they used this power to contest the rich and to fight authority. At other times they used it to impose their own point of view upon the dispossessed.

They organized themselves into secret societies or clubs, around journals or in parties. They were at the forefront of revolutions—on the Right as well as on the Left. They played key roles in revolutionary regimes, even to the point of turning themselves into a ruling class for new societies that arose according to the mold prepared by their ideas. They were ready for sacrifice: They were exiled, persecuted, imprisoned, tortured, killed, excluded, censured, deported, stripped of their nationality, and banned. At the same time they were ready to theorize the need for iron organizations that would be completely centralized and vertical, panopticons from whose control room they could see and make decisions about everything. There were intellectual leaders who were suspicious about intellectuals in general insofar as they did not show perfect readiness to abandon specific ways of seeing for the sake of the historic task that knowledge and the power that knowledge gave had placed in their hands. And they believed only a very few people could be leaders in a process of social change, while the led would have to submit to the process by force of argument or education, or by force itself. They insulted each other, went after each other, argued with each other, or chose to ignore each other even though they all belonged to the same general group.

They had a passion tied to the universal, to the rights of man and of the citizen, and to the rights of the working class who had only fully to take on board its tasks to become the source of freedom for all the oppressed. The fact that their passion was tied to the universal obliged them to look askance at particularistic perspectives, which they considered to be either holdovers deriving from backwardness or the unnatural fruit of the enemy's operation in the terrain of the people. They believed that the parties of the political vanguard were indispensable given the conditions of the struggle for progress and revolution. They were also indispensable because you could not rely simply on the masses, and on their spontaneous participation expected in these struggles, to ensure development and progress.

They were counselors to princes, dictators, enlightened autocrats—to other intellectuals who had become politicians, to intellectual politicians, and to politicians who had little to do with the world of ideas. They spoke for the People, for the Nation, for the World's Dispossessed, for the Oppressed Races, and for Minorities. When they addressed these interlocutors they thought they were transmitting a truth that they had discovered but that no one else would discover by their own free means alone. As a result they felt that they were Representatives, men and women who stood up and spoke *instead of* other men and women. And, as a result, they put their trust in the idea that this representation, this role of saying what others could not or knew not how to say, was one of their duties. This was a duty consequent upon knowledge. Their duty was to free everyone else from the fetters that prevented them from thinking and acting. And in the meantime, so long as this new consciousness had yet to be implanted within those who were to take it up in the future, they spoke in their name. They believed themselves to be the keepers of truths that had to be transmitted, generalized, disseminated, and imposed over and against error.

They felt that they were heroes, guides, and legislators. Many of them thought that their transformative mission was also a pedagogic mission and that society could be shaped so long as knowledge colonized all the social spaces that had seemed hitherto bereft of knowledge. Educating the uneducated came to be a mission taken up by intellectuals who then likewise carried over to nation-states this program of ideal betterment for the people. Still, at times they admired the people's "spontaneous" virtues when evident among peasants and the marginalized, though it was true that only their own expert gaze could identify them as virtues. They discovered strengths that those whose strengths these were had never realized, and they pointed out wisdom in those who did not consider themselves wise.

They founded their power in knowledge. They thought that the dissemination of knowledge was a source of freedom. For a long time it passed them by that knowledge could also be an instrument of social control. But then *no one* in their position denounced the fact that knowledge could be an instrument of social control.

Philosophers, moralists, writers, and artists all spoke up for an oppressed people in the face of those who had power. They spoke directly to the oppressed to teach them the means by which to break free of their chains. And they spoke to each other, as part of a long conversation now centuries old, about whether it was right to speak to the powerful or possible to speak to the oppressed, and about what to say in either case. They thought that they could address society and they thought that they could gain a hearing. For a long time they were listened to, respected, and consulted (albeit for that very reason, they were also subject to repression). They judged and denounced many atrocities, even if ideology or loyalty to old loyalties prevented them from judging and denouncing others.

Many artists had little respect for the limits of their office or the particularity of their calling. They were intellectuals, and they believed that art had something to say to society. They believed they provided an echo reverberating through the epoch, and that they were ambassadors for beauty to the masses who might at times recognize it and at times be blinded by its splendor. They were society's mirror or at least they wanted their work to be a mirror held up to whatever path people might think of taking. Like no one else (except perhaps saints) they explored the limits of experience, of the permissible, and of morality. They criticized customs and declared themselves to be above them. For this, many were imprisoned, confined in mental institutions, or reduced to abject poverty. But there were others who reigned like stars in the salons, the theaters, and the newspapers.

They thought that the public was an enlightened community of equals and that their work alone would win this audience over. They also thought that their audience was a pack of mediocre and philistine bourgeois, interested only in business and personal pleasure, an object of contempt for any true artist. At times they imagined women to be more sensitive and better prepared to understand art. At other times they declared that women were absolutely unreachable, and dreamed that they were angels or devils engulfed in their own sensuality, threatening to corrode the ideal and the strength of will necessary for beauty. They wrote for the People and for the Nation, thinking that their writing was what built the People or the Nation. They only wrote for their peers, showing contempt for any audience. They wrote looking for acclaim and they also wrote with the idea that they would not be read for many years to come. Some wrote with eternity in mind and others only believed in the worth of their work if it gained recognition in the present. They thought that they interpreted taste as part of a democratic community of peers, but they also thought that their work was the most definitive of departures or breaks from what their peers and the rest of the world judged art to be.

They held the past in contempt, argued with tradition, accepted it only to betray it, and also simply ignored it.

They compared themselves to the political vanguards, believing they were art's avant-garde. Here is where they produced this century's most impressive cultural achievements, by breaking with established taste, with accepted morality, and with the idea of art itself. They felt they were isolated, misunderstood, and rejected, and at the same time they believed that what they did held the keys to the future. Some elite groups adopted them, while the new mass art and cinema executives courted them. They took part in modernity's decisive battles, in which everything was said and everything that had been said before was questioned. They were both on their own and also hoping to take art to the very limits of life itself. They felt themselves part of history and supported revolutions, they fought against war and they made war, they united in a terrible embrace with political vanguards, and when they withdrew from this embrace they were repudiated or persecuted by the same regimes that they had earlier supported.

Some were radically intransigent to the point of no longer understanding the culture in which they lived. Others accommodated themselves to changing circumstances and sought out the comfort of power, popularity, and wealth. Some even went in both of these directions almost simultaneously.

They lived out the dilemmas involved in their being artists, philosophers, and intellectuals. They took force and legitimacy from the fact that they were different and were thus able to speak to society and to whole peoples. Yet they also criticized this illusion and indicated that their legitimacy was just an ornamental fiction serving to maintain established positions.

They felt that they were free in the face of any kind of power. They courted all sorts of powers. They were enthusiastic about the great revolutions, and they were also their first victims. *They are the intellectuals.* But this is a category whose very existence has become problematic today.

To return to the past is impossible. What has been, has been. Perhaps this is one of the few of modernity's lessons that are still relevant. We could only agree to a nostalgic trip around the gallery in which the past two centuries' great intellectual figures are arrayed if we understood it as a chance to peruse a tradition now finished and superseded by events. And yet the function of criticism—one function among many exercised by intellectuals and avant-gardes—still calls out powerfully. We have not seen the disappearance of the injustices that fired up challenges to absolute power and to forms of legitimacy based in either despotic authority or the concentration of wealth.

The societies that arise within this late modernity, that for shorthand we call postmodernity, are far from realizing an egalitarian, democratic ideal. The final collapse of actually existing socialist regimes sets the scene for a paleo-futurist nightmare on a massive scale, with the resurgence of racist nationalisms accompanied by the silencing and discrediting of any voice set on salvaging any value for the present from dreams of the past. Capitalism is living out its third, scientific and technical, revolution within the framework of societies that are fractured along the lines marked by poverty and turned upside down by the growth of individualist ideologies that refuse a notion of solidarity. Whereas the wealth of the countries of the core allows for compensatory policies on the part of the State and for social movements to intervene significantly in the public sphere, in the countries of the periphery the rapidly

approaching end of the century has to show for itself less cultural and social diversity than the intolerable difference between misery and wealth.

There can be no nostalgic return to images of what seemed
just and right in the past, but nor can we settle for uncritical
conformity with what emerges from the breakdown of these
images. The figure of the intellectual—as artist, philosopher, or
thinker—produced by classical modernity, has now entered
terminal decline. But there is still a call for some of the functions that such figures considered their own. Reality may have
changed (and therefore may no longer take legislators or
prophets to be its guides), but it has not changed so much that
it does not cry out for some of the lost intellectual functions.
Reality has not changed so much as to render useless what was
a central part of intellectual practice over the past two centuries, by which I mean the critique of what now exists, the free
and anticonformist spirit, the absence of fear before the powerful, and the sense of solidarity with those who are victims.

It may seem that there are few calling out for interventions
on the part of intellectuals, and that there are few intellectuals
ready to heed such cries, in part because memories are still
fresh of the errors committed earlier this century by the political vanguards (who constituted an intellectual style par excellence). What is more, we have learned the lessons of the great
successful mobilizations over the past few decades. Feminism,
human rights movements, and ethnic and cultural minorities
have taught us to value difference as a source of cultural
wealth, and this lesson fits badly with the absolutist vocation
and strong abstract tension associated with intellectuals in the
past. Moreover, in an environment encouraging us to remain
unstressed and distant, the heroic gestures of the intellectual as
saint or prophet seem especially discordant when compared to
this epoch's muted melody. We live in a "desensitized environment" (it has been said) in which declarations of principle are
only so much untimely thunder.

Moreover, no one wants to take on the risks involved in
dramatic ruptures. The myth of revolution has shown its sinis-

ter side and we have seen how historical breaks, once fanta-
sized to be clean incisions within the order of time, in fact turn
out to produce scars that keep alive the past's most sinister aspects. No one wants to abandon what, we can truthfully say,
has been gained in recent times: respect for difference, pluralism, and the principle of relativism. We hear it said that if intellectuals really want to have an effect within society, they
should keep their critical distance to the absolute minimum, to
avoid any overly spectacular separation from the community
to which they are directing their efforts. The model of heroic
intervention, put forward by the avant-gardes, does not interpellate anyone, either because society has left its ideals (the
driving force of heroism) so far behind, or because it is now
possible to produce various changes without material violence
or sainthood's symbolic violence, without the prophet's soli-
tude, and without the enlightened guide and his or her authority. Whatever the precise reason may be, the fact is that no one
is looking for intellectuals to adopt a heroic model.

What is more, even those who were once considered to be intellectuals are now the first to reject the role, and not only after
carrying out some in-depth critique of traditional modern intellectuals' heroic elitism. This rejection also arises from the success that public institutions have had in co-opting those who
have the kind of knowledge needed to carry out critique in general. Public intellectuals, that is to say the men and women
whose stage was once the public sphere, have in their thousands
now entered a very specific public space: academia. And here
they work not so much as intellectuals but rather as experts.

Experts are just like traditional intellectuals insofar as the
base upon which they build power is their mastery over a field
of knowledge or technique. Experts as such constitute a new
dominant class faction wherever knowledge is an integral
part of social production or of the production of the social.
Their influence increases proportionally as the set of knowledges required to produce decisions become every day more
and more complex. Experts, in their role as experts, tend to
demarcate the limits of the possible, and their opinions (which,

because they are authenticated by science and technology, appear to be free of any ideological bias) define long-term policy choices. In an environment in which everyone celebrates the end of ideology, experts embody the shape of history to come by guaranteeing pragmatism and by founding a new form of political realism. They make up the State bureaucracies that, in many countries, now have priority over political and governmental loyalties. They constitute the State's technical and administrative source of continuity and, like the State, they consider themselves to be above social groups and above their interests. They speak in the name of a technical knowledge that, like money, leaves no smell.

Experts coexisted with traditional intellectuals for decades, though each group distrusted the other, and not without reason. Today the battle appears to have been won by the experts, although in that their self-presentation denies that they bring with them values that might transcend the sphere of their particular expertise, they likewise fail to acknowledge the political and social results of their activity within that sphere. Naturally, the distinction between intellectuals and experts is a subtle one. The demands of his position within the political structure entail that an expert who becomes Economics minister needs a discourse to cover not only technical feasibility but also the question of what is deemed socially desirable. In such cases, experts have to offer us theories of good government, which are hardly short of general principles and which can be quite as fundamentalist as the theories offered by the old political vanguards, if not more so.

But alongside the Economics minister, within academia and in the State apparatus, are thousands of experts who consider what they do to be *apolitical*, even though they are in fact forever acting politically. Moreover, they regard their form of knowledge to be something like private property and as such untouched by ideology or questions of interest. These experts are women and men who belong to an administrative and scientific bureaucracy whose stability is assured in the countries of the center but whose fortunes in countries such as ours are

more closely linked to the ups and downs of the political process even if, on the whole, it tends to gain strength under
democracy. Aided by the faith people place in science and
technology (perhaps today, along with New Age religion, the
prime sources of the belief that flows toward the mass media's
lymphatic system), experts believe, first, in their own value
neutrality and, second, that a central part of their mission is to
protect this same neutrality. They give their expert opinion
from the seats of academe or from government aircraft carriers
and their opinion, *precisely* because it is an expert's opinion,
because it is considered to be above whatever interests are in
dispute, acquires an aura of objectivity.

The mass media (and especially print journalism) helps sew
the net together a little more by assigning objectivity to techno-
scientific practice and hence enabling expert judgments to seem
objective. An expert is, by definition, *expert in something,* in
some area of knowledge concerning society, art, nature, the
body, or subjectivity. The more objectivity wanted to vouch
for her opinions, the more an expert has to base these opinions
in a specific and limited field of knowledge: she should plow,
sow, and harvest but the one fruit, and respect the limits within
which others do their own plowing, sowing, and harvesting.

For decades philosophy has given up on any project to bring
together what is produced in these little plots of knowledge,
while it has been centuries since religion was last in a position
to convince any but its most fervent supporters that it could
achieve such a synthesis. We live in secular societies, but secu-
larism's radicality, which makes both ideological pluralism and
cultural relativism possible, also confronts us with a turning
point where we can find no certain terrain on which to base a
sense of value. And experts are the ones who, inadvertently for
the most part, have brought us this uprooting of all foundations. They regard technology as neutral, right up until some
catastrophe, some Chernobyl or Hiroshima, comes about. This
is clearly enough the case today, when we see the questions that
genetics poses to morality only beginning to be addressed.
Setting aside the churches, which have taken a set position, we

live in a world that has lost its moorings, and that oscillates between the position that anything goes on the one hand and
various attempts to agree, on the other hand, on a core set of
principles. Such principles would have to allow for the development of scientific research while also establishing limits that
the research itself calls out for, but that are not to be found in
any strictly scientific source. In claiming value neutrality, experts are less well equipped than ever at such turning points
where values are inextricably at stake.

By contrast, the very condition of existence of intellectuals
is (or was) the rejection of value neutrality. From the outset
they think that the dominant ideology represents the interests
of the dominant as the general interest. From the outset they
affirm the possibility of a rational foundation for determining
what is good for society. From the outset they believe that there
are certain values set out to be transcendent, to which social
order should have to adapt. Taking sides constitutes the very
motive force for intellectual practice. The clash of values is its
favored terrain.

There is no need to say once more, because everybody remembers, that taking sides brought about both the best and
the most sinister of intellectual practices over the past few centuries. A list would include the denunciations made in the
Dreyfus case, First World War pacifism, and antifascist and
anti-Nazi struggles. It would range from complacency toward
and complicity with Soviet authoritarianism, to the defense of
the Cuban revolution in the face of U.S. arrogance, but also
to the defense of the Cuban revolution when it imprisons gays,
former revolutionaries, and dissident intellectuals. It would include the campaigns against the Vietnam war but also the later
failure to look with a critical eye at the kind of society that
was built there. This taking of sides includes struggles against
anti-Semitism but also silence when faced with Arab racism,
denunciations of Arab fundamentalism but also silence when
faced with the excesses committed in anti-Arab wars, support
for the Algerian revolution but also the total absence of any
critique of the forms that revolution took or of the interne-

cine struggles staged there. We would have to mention not only the massive mobilization achieved by feminism, but also its narrow-minded interventions in some specifically, if not exclusively, North American situations. We would have to talk of the movement for African American rights but also of African American racism.

The list is endless and there is no way of reaching a mathematical formula by which to decide whether or not the intellectuals who took the lead in these often glorious episodes in fact made mistakes more often than they hit the right targets. When it comes down to it, judging any human practice from the perspective of what is strictly quantifiable is absurd. Let us suppose that, as intellectuals, Sartre made more mistakes than Raymond Aron, David Viñas more than Ernesto Sabato, Simone de Beauvoir fewer than Rossana Rossanda, Carlos Fuentes more than Octavio Paz, and Godard at least as many as Luigi Nono. Or the other way around. This is not the issue, unless you want to come up with some kind of balance sheet regarding an individual's trajectory (Sartre's or Paz's), but this is not the same as evaluating a social figure.

Do we need intellectuals? Is the presence of intellectuals inevitable given the benefits that experts, scientists, and artists find in the exercise of this function? Do we need a class of people whose job is to speak out about what does not concern them directly? What right does an Argentine have to speak about Vietnam, a Christian to speak about Jews or Arabs, a white to speak about blacks, a straight to speak about gays? Can you speak about the poor from a position of comfort or the rich when their riches have failed to trickle down to you? Is it best that only Cubans speak about Cuba, only Jews about the concentration camps, and only women about women? Are such specific discourses more appropriate, more powerful, or more authentic? Do we want a series of ghettos in which people speak only for what concerns them rather than open spaces in which anyone can speak out whatever their particular knowledge or interest, provided only they take into account other people's knowledges and interests? Is it better to have a society in which expert judgments are subject to the scrutiny of other experts alone, and where the arena in which decisions are evaluated is now particular rather than global? Does it guarantee greater pluralism when only geneticists can say how far genetic engineering should be taken, when only ethnic or cultural minorities can give an adequate account of what their rights should be, when only those who live in a given neighborhood can know what should be done in that neighborhood even though what they want affects a whole city, or when only the military can know whether or not a professional army is preferable to a citizen army?

If attempting to answer these questions still has any point, then the dual issue of who can speak and how they should speak has not been altogether eliminated, despite the crisis we see affecting the classical figure of the intellectual. We live in a society in which there has been a dispersion effect produced by individualism, by a retreat from the public sphere, by an inability to believe politicians and public institutions, by corruption on the part of politicians, judges, state functionaries, and capitalists, by the fact that the churches' preaching is overwhelmingly reactionary, by the worst mass media imaginable, and by the culture of the written word's decline and the crisis of the school as a space to redistribute symbolic benefits. This dispersion effect should not be misunderstood as implying some plurality of dynamic local centers, nor should an impoverishment of meaning on a global scale be confused with individual autonomy. Postmodernism's holy writ would suggest that in this situation of dispersion, the lack of strong social ties, the loss of community's traditional meanings, and the institution of new forms of community (communities of spectators, known as hermeneutic communities, or communities of consumers) are all universal phenomena that are to come accompanied by multipolarity, deterritorialization and nomadism, interest groups and cultural minorities' increasing autonomy, differences unfolding free of any competitive spirit, and the nonantagonistic coexistence of diverse value systems.

But by contrast in Argentina, at least, it has become quite

clear that the crisis in meaning on a global scale leads not so much to a new freedom of activity that would produce a multiplicity of particular meanings, but rather to a state of competition in which those who have more material and symbolic possessions are in a better position to impose the particularism that arises from their own specific interests. But even in countries in which social movements have managed to press their claims and be recognized institutionally by society, the loss of a "horizon of globality" produces strictly particularistic effects. These effects seldom find compensation in the still ill-defined project to construct a general front of particular interests (that lovely "rainbow coalition" to which Jesse Jackson referred when he was running to be nominated as presidential candidate in the United States). Yet while more progressive forces give up on setting their paths with any view to the global horizon, those sectors least interested in global transformation are in fact the ones who do still hold on to the idea that social problems are to be decided and negotiated on a global scale, even if they admit to particular solutions. The ability to situate particular conflicts within a general framework is a political device rooted in knowledge, ideas, ideals, and experience. Giving up on this device can only be done by simultaneously giving up on the project to bring about deep or lasting changes in society.

Clearly there is no point raising questions of no importance to anyone. The intellectual as prophet had an existence so removed from what was around him that his words became literally inaudible for those the prophet wished to alert to approaching disaster. The ability to listen and dialog needs *medium* distance to survive. Medium distance means neither the proximity of closed communities that can only accept their own discourses (and that are fiercely antirelativistic, fiercely fundamentalist), nor the distance, sometimes termed utopian, that posits a future and completely transformed world as the only setting from which the size of contemporary problems can be gauged. We need neither neotribalism nor imaginary worlds, because neither of these spaces allows us to construct an ideal sense of the public, of the res publica or public thing, on whose basis it might be possible to imagine "lucid actions" whose meaning would transcend the limits marked out by more particularistic interests, whether this be the particularism of money or gender, or one deriving from the exploitation of human beings or from the exploitation of nature. Within neotribalism or in imaginary worlds, those who do not belong or who do not deserve to belong are excluded from any solidarity and from the community of meaning. These are modernity's pariahs and exiles to whom postmodernity promises a corner in which subordinate identities pile up.

Traditional intellectuals will never again be the sole administrators for global issues. After the crisis in which they sank beneath the weight of their mistakes, and given the new environment that has no interest in rescuing the style with which they built their insights, there will be no restorative process by which their legitimacy returns or their lost authority is given back to them. However, neither those who see themselves as experts alone nor those who are today the new electronic intellectuals seem sufficiently prepared for the tasks that the present situation demands of us. Experts are unprepared because the laws of specialization accustom them only to thinking with their gaze focused on a single point, that of their specific area of knowledge and the specific interests with which, openly or otherwise, it is interlaced. The new electronic intellectuals, on the other hand, lack any knowledge other than that produced by the media, and the insufficiency of this becomes apparent at the point at which they themselves resort to expert opinion as part of a process of circular legitimation. Still, experts and electronic intellectuals alike are in this world to stay, and if this is the case they will be able to transform themselves according to this world's requirements. Nobody is excluded in advance from a perspective in which the gaze can focus simultaneously on the familiar and on the far horizon, on which is drawn a social landscape that finally, despite the increased breadth of this gaze, continues to include particularisms.

The most diverse determinisms (such as economic, technical, or media determinisms) may believe that history happens blindly, but history does not happen blindly, nor is it a process without a subject, nor is it a space from which freedom is absent. Ideas have as much weight today as do relations of force. The crisis of meaning has deprived us of unifying general ideas, but it has not deprived of ideas those who seem to move blindly in accord with their most immediate interests, nor has it deprived those who seem to defend one single idea that marks them out and makes them unique. Nor even has this crisis deprived those who are in government, and who decide the fate of nations, of their general ideas. And ideas held by experts, however much they may appear to affect but one dimension of the real, unleash processes that have consequences upon other dimensions. There are a few facts of social life that affect all of us, even given the absolutely justified critique of a "hard" concept of totality and its deterministic kernel. And yet new determinisms, both optimistic and pessimistic, proliferate, and they include the technological optimism that sees in every scientific advance an auspicious change in our standard of living. On the other side is the technological pessimism maintained by many strains of the environmental movement, that regards every scientific development as a threat to the planet's natural diversity. There is also neoliberalism and its view that the market is the only instance of totalization, and its faith that the market can produce a society stripped to its essentials precisely as an effect of what goes on in the market. Finally, there is the neopopulism without either People or Nation, that considers public opinion as constructed through polls to constitute a globality whose diktats allow no appeal and are invariably correct.

Yet in a democratic society there are questions that have to be put to and debated by the citizen body: Is it just? Is it more egalitarian? Who is harmed by my action? Who apart from myself benefits? The answers to these questions would not promise a catechism for good government, but in a world that is increasingly homogenous and increasingly individualist (a fatal combination of qualities), they would at least allow us to take other people's points of view into account. This would be the pluralist consequence of considering general questions. Without a general perspective, pluralism is particularistic rather than tolerant. Questions that force us to discuss equality and justice constitute an intellectual limit against social developments that prompt us to act without any understanding of what might be a perspective on the common good. Of course, we all know that the concept of the common good is problematic, and that in the last hundred years Marxism has subjected it to critique and denounced it as an ideological fiction under whose cover those who had sufficient economic and political power were able to put forward what they wanted and impose their own interests simply in the name of the common good. We all also know that it is difficult (many would say impossible) to define the common good in societies that have lost any transcendent grounding and that therefore cannot agree on what might ground the common good. We no longer have gods to point out to mortals the nature of good. This is the problem, and we cannot escape it along the paths of particularism, nor can we be saved from uncertainty by postmodernism's dogma concerning the old certainties' explosion.

This is our condition. We desire justice, equality, and liberty for all, and we have learned that it is absurd to postpone the realization of these values until the end of history (whatever the name of the utopia identified with this end of history). And yet the knowledge that injustice in the present cannot be justified in the name of a justice to come, and the knowledge that the promise of future freedoms ought not be invoked as a reason to damage the freedoms we have here and now, should not necessarily lead to a perspective tied only to the moment, in which hedonistic attachment to the present blinds us to everyday inequalities. An "intelligent action" worthy of the name is so not simply as a function of its immediate results, though its immediate results should maintain some articulated relation to whatever mediated ends may follow. Here dwell the dilemmas that are attendant upon the practice of politics and the attempt to build society. Particularism and hedonistic attachments to the present fail to gauge their actions with reference to globality in the present or to a future horizon. As if caught in a pincer movement, they ignore both other people and historical time. Absolute relativism, in judging that distinct groups' values are equally close to God (now that, finally, there is no God and no Truth), abandons society's workings to rationalities that can be extremely particular and, often enough, even incompatible with the very principles of relativism and of universal respect for other values. When everybody is out for his or her own happiness, and whatever the theory may say, the result is a more unequal and unhappier society.

In this environment, the argument that we need a general discussion on the level of ideas cannot be put down to traditional intellectuals' vanity, or to the illegitimate survival of covert Hegelians or Marxists staking their symbolic power on the reconstruction of some determined totality. Nor should we concede the production of general ideas to the one institution that, factory-like, turns them out in quantity, the mass media. Beneficiaries of the fact that modernity's great centers of ideological construction are now in tatters, and protected from any suspicion of bias, the media provide us with almost all the social fictions that we consume. They present themselves as constituting a space that is general, open, and pluralist. The media's viewing public grant that this is the case precisely because they do not grant politics, or any other sphere, the capacity to put out a message that would be both inclusive and apparently true to life.

Given the complexity of contemporary society (and the still greater complexity of peripheral societies such as our own), taking political decisions requires a huge number of ultrasophisticated forms of knowledge. Such knowledges only enter into media circulation as ghostly reflections or lifeless quotations. And yet a familiarity with these forms of knowledge (especially those concerning society itself) is indispensable if what is wanted is to change what comes out of that society. Someone once commented that we live in one of the few countries of the world in which the explanations we are offered about economics are totally incomprehensible. If this is the case, it should come as no surprise that men and women judge the economy only in terms of the most immediate results that it yields for their own lives. The increasing difficulty people find in understanding these forms of knowledge and the loss of a sense of the general good are both effects of processes that go hand in hand. Society is more and more dependent upon information and communication when it comes to technology, yet there are some essential issues that are becoming more and more opaque. Hence the right to make decisions is ceded to experts and to their political bosses. At the same time, the revenge of popular common sense comes when these same politicians are adjudged to be hopelessly corrupt.

The emptying out of meaning has to do not only with the explosion within the present, but also with the shadow that accompanies it. It is also a question of the past, of the way in which history is now forgotten, in that our experience of time as "no longer historical time" is therefore also a form of experience that has no links with the past and makes no promises for the future. In the dissemination of meaning and the fragmentation of identity, it is not only the authority of tradition that founders. We also lose the anchors that would allow our lived experience of the present to be something more than simply one instant ever to be followed by another instant equally and homogeneously "present." We lose the anchors that allow us to experience the present as part of a project. The past no longer weighs upon the brain of the living, as the philosopher would have it; on the contrary, it has so little weight that it prevents us from imagining "the continuity of our own history."

The increasing speed of media rhetoric can be read as an allegory. We move at the pace of the abrupt shifts enabled by televisual zapping, in the sense that we lack the requisite memory (because memory is a function of taking your time and of handling density) that would establish connections between what has just happened and what is happening now. I am not talking about bringing back some historical romanticism that would find in the past the keys with which to explain every aspect of what we see here and now. Far from some idea of explanatory origin, what is at issue is tracing the scars (often still open) with which the past marks the present, and the debts that the present owes for injustices committed in a past that should be read for the duties, obligations, and rights yet to be realized in the present. The present should not face ever forward with the freedom of some Robinson Crusoe feeling he is the first person to set foot on his island. In this island of time in which we live, we need to be able to hear the voices that reach out from behind us. Nobody is free of responsibility, and responsibility is not simply a matter of future actions. We are as responsible for the past as we are for the future because, as Walter Benjamin pointed out, the past is the site of unfinished tasks and injustices that still need compensation. The attempt to cast our eyes only toward the future is a form of temporal hedonism. Those who want to criticize the present have to consider the past, and the past constitutes an intolerable legacy only if we simply accept it without subjecting it, too, to radical critique.

Our relation to history has to be *humanist*. Were it not for the historians, neither science nor technology would seem to have a history. Scientists have no interest in the history of science (perhaps because they refuse to read epistemology either). The idea of a culture made up of humanities and art seems frankly an archaism in a context in which the smallest changes in information technology or in genetics are celebrated for their prophetic consequences. And yet, just as Antonio Gramsci suggested to the Italian working class that they should refuse to allow the creation of purely professional schools in their name, so the idea of a humanist culture can be defended as a necessity rather than simply a luxury within techno-scientific culture.

In the space vacated by a society that entrusts art to specialists and that confines artists to ghettos of snobbery or to specialized fringes of the market, the media provide a parodic version of the humanities and of art. When Luciano Pavarotti bellows out a concert in an avenue one hundred yards wide, literally nothing is happening, beyond an abrupt rise in the sale of Pavarotti compact discs whose benefits, at least, go somewhat further than the huge international recording companies. What we see singing is but a phantom produced by the media. And yet, there is something going on because a melody, a chord from the orchestra, or a piercing note from the tenor all retain a trace of what it is to have an aesthetic experience. There is no reason to think that the enjoyable entertainment produced by these media phantoms is the only form of art that can be thrown at the masses. Up until the 1950s, and from time to time even now, the cinema succeeded in being the model of an innovative aesthetic that was also very much adapted to the very mass society that it was itself helping to construct. The question is not whether or not millions of people are going to see Godard's latest film, because that would be impossible. The question is whether or not millions of people have no other potential for aesthetic enjoyment than that provided by a dancer who jumps around a stage, barely visible a hundred yards in the distance, or by zapping's home montage.

Art offers an experience of limits. We have a civilization in which the collapse of traditional religions, the rise of New Age religions as some kind of consolation, the absolute sense of the present underpinned by the market, medical technology, and ideologies claiming to do away with temporality all insist on avoiding even the idea of death. Art stages this limit. There is no reason that would lead us to believe that millions of men and women should be excluded from such an experience, out of some principle of social inequality (albeit dressed up as a principle of tolerance). Of course no one would want to bring back a pedagogic paradigm whose program would be the aesthetic indoctrination of the multitudes. Rather what I am arguing is for incorporating art back into our reflections on culture, from where it has been dislodged by broad definitions of culture along anthropological lines. We are well aware—and by now it is hard these days to go against what has become common sense here—that everything is culture.

Yet there is something in the experience of art that makes it a moment of semantic and formal intensity different from that which results from cooking, sport, or the televisual continuum. It is true that every cultural manifestation is legitimate and that pluralism teaches us that they should all be equally respected. But not every cultural manifestation is in fact equal.

A culture has to be in a position to "name the differences that constitute it." If this naming does not happen, only aesthetic or intellectual elites will be destined to achieve the exercise of cultural freedom. For the freedom to enjoy culture's various levels to be open to all (though not all need choose it), it has to be backed by two sources of power: by the State, which can intervene to bring balance to the market, whose aesthetic betrays its relation to profit; and by a cultural critique that can free itself from the double bind of either neo-populist celebration of what we already have or an elitist perspective that undermines any possibility of articulating a democratic perspective.

Must cultural critique be, in the end, a discourse produced by and for intellectuals? It is hard to see any group that has the requisite skills to seize hold of the site from which this discourse can be articulated. Unlike in the past, when there were many who wanted to speak to the People, to the Nation, or to Society, few now long to win over these distant, imaginary, or uninterested interlocutors.

And yet this site of critique can be marked out, the problems we face call for us to intervene, and, what is more, reality allows for few alternatives. We can come up with new and better arguments by which to criticize the conformism that settles for what exists at present as though it were all that were possible, to criticize the eroticized celebration of power, to criticize self-congratulatory and indifferent quiescence, or to criticize cynicism, once used as a weapon with which to attack the powerful and now, it seems, aimed solely at those who want progress.

Critical thought is not a solution to this knot of problems. It is, only, a way of seeing things. The narrow door is still ajar.

Bibliography

Here I mention the books or articles that have helped me construct my own arguments, with which this text is in critical dialogue.

Beyond this bibliographical list, I would also like to thank Carlos Altamirano, Raúl Beceyro, Rafael Filippelli, Adrián Gorelik, and Federico Monjeau. Ricardo Ibarlucía thought that I should write this book, and let me know that he thought so.

Brief fragments of this book (on zapping, video games, and aesthetic value) appeared originally in *Punto de Vista* and *Página 30,* but are published here in revised and expanded form.

1. Abundance and Poverty

City

Benjamin, Walter. *Illuminations.* Edited and introdced by Hannah Arendt. Translated by Harry Zohn. New York: Harcourt, Brace and World, 1968.

Dorfles, Gillo. *Il feticcio quotidiano.* Milan: Feltrinelli, 1988.

García Canclini, Néstor. *Hybrid Cultures: Strategies for Entering and Leaving Modernity.* Translated by Christopher L. Chiappari and Silvia L. López. Foreword by Renato Rosaldo. Minneapolis: University of Minnesota Press, 1995.

Jameson, Fredric. *Postmodernism, or, The Cultural Logic of Late Capitalism.* Durham, NC: Duke University Press, 1991.

Schorske, Carl. "La idea de ciudad en el pensamiento europeo: de

Voltaire a Spengler." Accompanying document distributed with
Punto de Vista 30 (July 1987).

Silvestri, Graciela, and Adrián Gorelik. "Paseo de compras: un recorrido
por la decadencia urbana de Buenos Aires." *Punto de Vista* 37 (July
1990): 23–28.

Market

Barker, Francis. *The Tremulous Private Body*. London: Methuen, 1984.

Benjamin, Walter. "Eduard Fuchs: Collector and Historian." In *One-
Way Street and Other Writings*. Translated by Edmund Jephcott and
Kingsley Shorter. London: Verso, 1997, 340–86.

Chaney, David. *Fictions of Collective Life: Public Drama in Late
Modern Culture*. London: Routledge, 1993.

Formations of Pleasure. London: Routledge, 1983.

Hebdige, Dick. *Subculture: The Meaning of Style*. London: Methuen,
1979.

———. *Hiding in the Light*. London: Routledge, 1988.

Youth

Alabarces, Pablo. *Entre gatos y violadores: el rock nacional en la cultura
argentina*. Buenos Aires: Colihue, 1993.

Arcand, Bernard. *The Jaguar and the Anteater: Pornography Degree
Zero*. Translated by Wayne Grady. London: Verso, 1993.

Barthes, Roland. *The Fashion System*. Translated by Matthew Ward and
Richard Howard. New York: Hill and Wang, 1983.

Fatela, Joao, and Patrick Mignon. "Le Rock pour ne pas dire 'c'est fini.'"
Esprit 33–34 (September 1992): 182–88.

Hebdige, Dick. *Subculture: The Meaning of Style*. London: Methuen,
1979.

———. *Hiding in the Light*. London: Routledge, 1988.

Ibarlucía, Ricardo. "Once tesis sobre el rock." Manuscript. Buenos Aires,
1993.

Mignon, Patrick. "Existe-t-il une 'culture rock'?" Interview conducted by
Pierre Bouretz. *Esprit* 193 (July 1993): 140–50.

No. Youth supplement to *Página 12*, Buenos Aires.

Olalquiaga, Celeste. *Megalopolis: Contemporary Cultural Sensibilities*.
Minneapolis: University of Minnesota Press, 1992.

Ramos, Laura, and Cynthia Lejbowicz. *Corazones en llamas: historias
del rock argentino en los '80*. Buenos Aires: Aguilar/Clarín, 1991.

Sí. Youth supplement to *Clarín*, Buenos Aires.

Vila, Pablo. "Rock nacional: crónicas de la resistencia juvenil." In *Los
nuevos movimientos sociales*. Vol. 1., *Mujeres. Rock nacional*. Edited
by Elizabeth Jelin, 83–148. Buenos Aires: CEAL, 1985.

————. "El rock, música argentina contemporánea." *Punto de Vista* 30 (July–October 1987): 23–29.

Video Games

Calabrese, Omar. *Neo-Baroque: A Sign of the Times*. Translated by Charles Lambert. Foreword by Umberto Eco. Princeton: Princeton University Press, 1992.

Consumer Guide Editors. *How to Win at Video Games*. New York: Pocket, 1982.

Fiske, John. *Reading the Popular*. Boston: Unwin Hyman, 1989.

Mongin, Olivier. *La peur du vide: essai sur les passions démocratiques*. Paris: Seuil, 1991.

2. The Waking Dream

Amiel, Vincent. "Des images de mondes superposés." *Esprit* 10 (October 1991).

Arfuch, Leonor. "Reality shows: cinismo y política." Photocopy, 1993.

————. *La interioridad pública: la entrevista como género*. Buenos Aires: Universidad de Buenos Aires, Facultad de Ciencias Sociales, 1992.

"Autismo tecno." Supplement to *Futuro, Página 12* (October 30, 1993).

Barbero, Jesús Martín. *Communication, Culture, and Hegemony: From the Media to Mediations*. Translated by Elizabeth Fox and Robert A. White. London: Sage, 1993.

Baudrillard, Jean. *Fatal Strategies*. London: Pluto, 1990.

Bürger, Peter. *The Decline of Modernism*. Translated by Nicholas Walker. University Park, PA: Pennsylvania State University Press, 1992.

Calabrese, Omar. *Neo-Baroque: A Sign of the Times*. Translated by Charles Lambert. Foreword by Umberto Eco. Princeton: Princeton University Press, 1992.

Casetti, Francesco, and Roger Odin. "De la paléo à la néotélévision." *Communications* 51 (1990): 9–24.

Chaney, David. *Fictions of Collective Life: Public Drama in Late Modern Culture*. London: Routledge, 1993.

Coste-Cerdan, Nathalie, and Alain Le Diberder. *La télévision*. Paris: La Découverte, 1986.

Dorfles, Gillo. *Il feticcio quotidiano*. Milan: Feltrinelli, 1988.

Eco, Umberto. *Travels in Hyperreality*. London: Pan, in association with Secker and Warburg, 1986.

————. *The Open Work*. Translated by Anna Concogni. Introduction by David Robey. Cambridge, MA: Harvard University Press, 1989.

García Canclini, Néstor. "La cultura bajo la regresión neoconservadora; Una modernización que atrasa." Photocopy. 1993.

Landi, Oscar. *Devórame otra vez: qué hizo la televisión con la gente, qué hace la gente con la televisión.* Buenos Aires: Planeta, 1992.

Mangone, Carlos. *Tinelli.* Buenos Aires: La Marca, 1992.

McLuhan, Marshall. *The Gutenberg Galaxy: The Making of Typographic Man.* Toronto: University of Toronto Press, 1962.

Rinesi, Eduardo. *Mariano.* Buenos Aires: La Marca, 1992.

Sandler, Irving. *The Triumph of American Painting: A History of Abstract Expressionism.* New York: Praeger, 1970.

Schmucler, Héctor. "La política como mercado o la desventura de la ética." *Política y comunicación: ¿hay un lugar para la política en la cultura mediática?* Edited by Héctor Schmucler and María Cristina Mata. Buenos Aires: Universidad Nacional de Córdoba/Catálogos, 1992.

"Un nouvel age télévisuel?" Special Dossier. *Esprit* 188 (January 1993): 5–81.

Vattimo, Gianni. *The Transparent Society.* Translated by David Webb. Baltimore, MD: The Johns Hopkins University Press, 1992.

Vezzetti, Hugo. "El sujeto psicológico en el universo massmediático." *Punto de Vista* 47 (December 1993): 22–30.

Williams, Raymond. *Television: Technology and Cultural Form.* London: Fontana, 1974.

3. Popular Cultures, Old and New

Auyero, Javier. *Otra vez en la vía: notas e interrogantes sobre la juventud de sectores populares.* Buenos Aires: Espacio/GECUSO, 1993.

Barbero, Jesús Martín. *Communication, Culture, and Hegemony: From the Media to Mediations.* Translated by Elizabeth Fox and Robert A. White. London: Sage, 1993.

———. "Innovacíon tecnológica y transformación cultural." *Telos* 9 (1987): 24–31.

Bourdieu, Pierre. "Did You Say Popular?" Translated by Gino Raymond. In *Language and Symbolic Power.* Edited and introduced by John B. Thompson, 90–102. Cambridge, MA: Harvard University Press, 1991.

Chaney, David. *Fictions of Collective Life: Public Drama in Late Modern Culture.* London: Routledge, 1993.

De Certeau, Michel. *The Practice of Everyday Life.* Berkeley: University of California Press, 1984.

Ford, Aníbal. *Desde la orilla de la ciencia: ensayos sobre identidad, cultura y territorio.* Buenos Aires: Puntosur, 1987.

García Canclini, Néstor. *Hybrid Cultures: Strategies for Entering and Leaving Modernity.* Translated by Christopher L. Chiappari and Silvia L. López. Foreword by Renato Rosaldo. Minneapolis: University of Minnesota Press, 1995.

————. "La cultura bajo la regresión neoconservadora; Una modernización que atrasa." Photocopy. 1993.

————. *Transforming Modernity: Popular Culture in Mexico.* Translated by Lidia Lozano. Austin: University of Texas Press, 1993.

Grignon, Claude, and Jean-Claude Passeron. *Le savant et le populaire: misérabilisme et populisme en sociologie et en littérature.* Paris: Seuil, 1989.

Gutiérrez, Leandro, and Luis Alberto Romero. "Sociedades barriales, bibliotecas populares y cultura de los sectores populares: Buenos Aires 1920–1935." *Desarollo Económico* 113 (April/June 1989): 33–63.

Hoggart, Richard. *The Uses of Literacy.* London: Chatto and Windus, 1957.

Lehmann, David. "Prolegómeno a las revoluciones religiosas en América Latina." *Punto de Vista* 43 (August 1992): 35–41.

Ortiz, Renato. *A moderna tradição brasileira.* São Paulo: Brasiliense, 1988.

Richard, Nelly. *La estratificación de los márgenes.* Santiago de Chile: F. Zegers, 1989.

Romero, Luis Alberto. *Los sectores populares urbanos como sujetos históricos.* Buenos Aires: PEHE-SA-CISEA, 1987.

Rowe, William, and Vivian Schelling. *Memory and Modernity: Popular Culture in Latin America.* London: Verso, 1991.

Rubinich, Lucas. *Tomar la cultura del pueblo, bajar la cultura al pueblo: dos nociones de la acción cultural.* Buenos Aires: Fundación del Sur/GECUSO, 1992.

Schwarz, Roberto. "Discutindo com Alfredo Bosi." Review of Bosi, *Dialéctica da colonização. Novos Estudos* 36 (July 1993): 9–22.

Semán, Pablo. "Pentecostales: un cristianismo inesperado." *Punto de Vista* 47 (December 1993): 26–30.

4. The Place of Art

Snapshots

Juan José Saer, Sergio Chejfec, Eduardo Stupía, and Daniel Samoilovich are my friends, as was Juan Pablo Renzi until his disappearance in 1992. These are the people from whom I have taken the characteristics described in these "snapshots," taking certain liberties for which they have not given permission, but which they will, I am sure, understand. Rafael Filippelli also has much to do with all these snapshots.

Values and the Market

Adorno, T. W. *Aesthetic Theory.* Translated by C. Lenhardt and edited by Gretel Adorno. London: Routledge, 1984.

Bauman, Zygmunt. *Intimations of Postmodernity.* London: Routledge, 1992.

Benjamin, Andrew. *Art, Mimesis, and the Avant-Garde.* London: Routledge, 1991.

Bourdieu, Pierre. *The Rules of Art: Genesis and Structure of the Literary Field.* Stanford, CA: Stanford University Press, 1995.

Bürger, Peter. *Theory of Avant-Garde.* Translated by Michael Shaw. Minneapolis: University of Minnesota Press, 1984.

Calinescu, Matei. *Faces of Modernity: Avant-Garde, Decadence, Kitsch.* Bloomington: Indiana University Press, 1977.

Foster, Hal. *The Anti-Aesthetic: Essays in Postmodern Cultures.* Port Townsend, WA: Bay Press, 1983.

———. *Recodings: Art, Spectacle, Cultural Politics.* Seattle, WA: Bay Press, 1985.

Franco, Jean. "Going Public: Reinhabiting the Private." In *On Edge: The Crisis of Contemporary Latin American Culture.* Edited by George Yúdice, Jean Franco, and Juan Flores, 65–84. Minneapolis: University of Minnesota Press, 1992.

Gablik, Suzi. *Has Modernism Failed?* New York: Thames and Hudson, 1985.

Gramuglio, María Teresa. "La summa de Bourdieu." *Punto de Vista* 47 (December 1993): 38–42.

Grignon, Claude, and Jean-Claude Passeron. *Le savant et le populaire: misérabilisme et populisme en sociologie et en littérature.* Paris: Seuil, 1989.

Lyotard, Jean-François. "Philosophy and Painting in the Age of Their Experimentation: Contribution to an Idea of Postmodernity." Translated by Maria Minich Brewer and Daniel Brewer. *Camera Obscura* (1984): 110–25.

———. "The Sublime and the Avant-Garde." Translated by Lisa Liebmann, with Geoff Bennington and Marian Hobson. In *The Lyotard Reader.* Edited by Andrew Benjamin, 196–211. Oxford: Blackwell, 1989.

Molino, Jean. "L'art aujourd'hui." *Esprit* 173 (July–August 1991): 72–108.

Monjeau, Federico. "En torno del progreso." *Lulú, revista de teorías y técnicas musicales* 3 (April 1992): 9–16.

Robbins, Bruce, ed. *Intellectuals: Aesthetics, Politics, Academics.* Minneapolis: University of Minnesota Press, 1990.

Ross, Andrew. *No Respect: Intellectuals and Popular Culture.* London: Routledge, 1989.

Saavedra, Guillermo. *La curiosidad impertinente: entrevistas con narradores argentinos.* Rosario: Beatriz Viterbo, 1993.

Schwarz, Roberto. "Discutindo com Alfredo Bosi." Review of Bosi, *Dialéctica da colonização*. *Novos Estudos* 36 (July 1993): 9–22.

―――. *Ao vencedor as batatas: forma literária e processo social nos inícios do romance brasileiro*. São Paulo: Duas Cidades, 1977.

Todorov, Tzvetan. *Literature and Its Theorists: A Personal View of Twentieth-Century Criticism*. Translated by Catherine Porter. Ithaca, NY: Cornell University Press, 1987.

Vattimo, Gianni. *The Transparent Society*. Translated by David Webb. Baltimore, MD: The Johns Hopkins University Press, 1992.

Williams, Raymond. *Marxism and Literature*. Oxford: Oxford University Press, 1977.

5. Intellectuals

Alberoni, Francesco, and Salvatore Veca. *L'altruismo e la morale*. Milan: Garzanti, 1988.

Altamirano, Carlos. "Los intelectuales, de Alfonsín a Menem" (reporting by G. Saavedra). *Clarín* (July 12, 1992).

―――. "Hipótesis de lectura (sobre el tema de los intelectuales en la obra de Tulio Halperín Donghi)." *Punto de Vista* 44 (November 1992): 38–42.

Aronowitz, Stanley. "On Intellectuals." In *Intellectuals: Aesthetics, Politics, Academics*. Edited by Bruce Robbins, 3–56. Minneapolis: University of Minnesota Press, 1990.

Bauman, Zygmunt. *Legislators and Interpreters: On Modernity, Postmodernity, and Intellectuals*. Ithaca, NY: Cornell University Press, 1987.

―――. *Intimations of Postmodernity*. London: Routledge, 1992.

Benjamin, Andrew. *Art, Mimesis, and the Avant-Garde*. London: Routledge, 1991.

Bourdieu, Pierre. "No hay democracia efectiva sin un contrapoder político." Interview. *Clarín* (July 30, 1992).

Castoriadis, Cornelius. "Le délabrement de l'occident." Interview conducted by Oliver Mongin, Joël Roman, and Ramin Jahanbegloo. *Esprit* 177 (December 1991): 36–54.

Foucault, Michel. *The Archaeology of Knowledge*. Translated by A. M. Sheridan Smith. London: Tavistock, 1972.

―――. *Microfísica del poder*. Madrid: La Piqueta, 1978.

Gouldner, Alvin. *The Future of Intellectuals and the Rise of the New Class*. New York: Continuum, 1979.

Gramsci, Antonio. *Selections from the Prison Notebooks*. Edited and translated by Quintin Hoare and Geoffrey Nowell Smith. London: Lawrence and Wishart, 1971.

Haraway, Donna. "A Manifesto for Cyborgs: Science, Technology, and

Socialist Feminism in the 1980s." *Socialist Review* 80 (March–April 1985): 65–107.

Janicaud, Dominique. "La double méprise: les lettres dans la civilisation scientifico-technique." *Esprit* 185 (October 1992): 71–79.

Mongin, Olivier. "Une mémoire sans histoire? Vers une autre relation à l'histoire." *Esprit* 190 (March/April 1993): 102–13.

Nora, Pierre. *Realms of Memory: Rethinking the French Past.* New York: Columbia University Press, 1996.

"La pensée en 1993." Dossier published in *Nouvel Observateur* 1508 (September 30, 1993).

Ricoeur, Paul. *Lectures on Ideology and Utopia.* Edited by George Taylor. New York: Columbia University Press, 1986.

Ross, Andrew. "Defenders of the Faith and the New Class." In *Intellectuals: Aesthetics, Politics, Academics.* Edited by Bruce Robbins, 101–32. Minneapolis: University of Minnesota Press, 1990.

Rossanda, Rossana. *Le altre: conversazioni a Radiotre sui rapporti tra donne e politica, libertà, fraternità, uguaglianza, democrazia, fascismo, resistenza, Stato, partito, rivoluzione, femminismo.* Milan: Bompiani, 1979.

Sartre, Jean-Paul. "A Plea for Intellectuals." In *Between Existentialism and Marxism.* London: New Left Books, 1974, 128–49.

Sigal, Silvia. *Intelectuales y poder en la década del setenta.* Buenos Aires: Puntosur, 1991.

Silvestri, Graciela. "La convención verde. Contra la naturalización ecologista de la vida urbana." *Punto de Vista* 48 (April 1994): 10–16.

Spivak, Gayatri Chakravorty. "Can the Subaltern Speak?" In *Marxism and the Interpretation of Culture.* Edited by Cary Nelson and Lawrence Grossberg, 271–313. Urbana: University of Illinois Press, 1988.

Walzer, Michael. *The Company of Critics: Social Criticism and Political Commitment in the Twentieth Century.* New York: Basic Books, 1988.

Williams, Raymond. *Towards 2000.* London: Chatto and Windus, 1983.

Yúdice, George. "Postmodernity and Transnational Capitalism in Latin America." In *On Edge: The Crisis of Contemporary Latin American Culture.* Edited by George Yúdice, Jean Franco, and Juan Flores, 1–28. Minneapolis: University of Minnesota Press, 1992.

Beatriz Sarlo, a prominent Latin American cultural critic, is professor of literature at the University of Buenos Aires. She has also taught at Columbia University, the University of California at Berkeley, the University of Minnesota, and Cambridge University. She is the author of *Borges: A Writer on the Edge,* among many books, and the cofounder of the journal *Punto de Vista.*

Jon Beasley-Murray is a lecturer in the Department of Spanish and Portuguese Studies and codirector of the Program in Latin American Cultural Studies at the University of Manchester, specializing in social theory and twentieth-century Latin American history and culture.